An Uncommon Heroine

Scarlett, Edna, Sula—
and More Than 20 Other
of the
Most Remarkable
Women in Literature

JAMIE COX ROBERTSON

Avon, Massachusetts

Dedicated to my mother, Barbara Jennell Cox
and my daughter, Sophia Jennell Robertson

Published by
Adams Media, a division of F+W Media, Inc.
57 Littlefield Street, Avon, MA 02322. U.S.A.
www.adamsmedia.com

ISBN 10: 1-4405-0417-2
ISBN 13: 978-1-4405-0417-4
eISBN 10: 1-4405-0878-X
eISBN 13: 978-1-4405-0878-3

Printed in the United States of America.

10   9   8   7   6   5   4   3   2   1

Library of Congress Cataloging-in-Publication Data
Robertson, Jamie Cox.
An uncommon heroine / Jamie Cox Robertson.
p. cm.
ISBN 978-1-4405-0417-4 — ISBN 978-1-4405-0878-3 (eBook)
1. Women in literature. 2. Characters and characteristics in literature. I. Title.
PN56.5.W64R63 2010
809'.933522—dc22
2010025718

This book is available at quantity discounts for bulk purchases.
For information, please call 1-800-289-0963.

Table of Contents

Introduction

I returned to the working world after a two-year hiatus and taught a couple of English classes at Suffolk University. As I prepared for one such class, I came across Truman Capote's *Breakfast at Tiffany's*, a novella about a carefree party girl named Holly Golightly. Rereading the book took me back fifteen years to the first time I taught college English and assigned the story to my class. I was twenty-four years old—barely older than my students. In my twenties, I thought of Holly as a self-centered girl who dated entirely too many men. But reading Capote's novel again so many years later caused me to see Holly Golightly in a completely different way than I did back then. Now I see a necessary rite of passage to her outrageousness and self-centeredness, and I think a woman's twenties is the perfect time to be whimsical and unpredictable. And besides, most girls are destined to make a lot of bad choices when it comes to men before ever finding the right one.

I got to thinking—would I see other women I had read about in a different light now that I was older, married, and had a daughter of my own? I decided to go back and reread a lot of great classic literature about women and see what I thought of those women now. I also decided to read some novels I had never read. *An Uncommon Heroine* is the result of all the reading—and rereading—that I did. Of course, this collection of novel excerpts cannot include every book about an unforgettable woman in fiction, but the women I've chosen are, to say the least, fascinating in their own right.

The women in this book are not the Eleanor Roosevelts or Marilyn Monroes of our world—they are mothers, daughters, lovers, and wives just like you and me. The writers who created them cut to the core of what it means to be a woman living on her own terms. The result is sometimes rewarding, other times regretful, but most of the time these heroines simply learn from their experiences and use that knowledge as they forge ahead into new challenges. That's the appeal for me. Hopefully, that will be the appeal for you too. But whatever you take away from this collection, I hope you will find these women's stories to be as enlightening, engaging, and thought-provoking as I have.

Anne Elliot

IN *PERSUASION* BY JANE AUSTEN

FIRST PUBLISHED IN: 1818

Who is she? A heartbroken woman who is given a second chance to prove she isn't so easily persuaded.

Her Story

Anne is the quiet, dutiful middle child in a family full of vain and flamboyant characters. To hear her father and sister talk, one would think Anne was a frumpy old woman with no interest in anything other than her books. Even worse, her family has given up on her ever finding a husband. But Anne's passion and desire to love run deeper than anyone in her family will ever know. She made a mistake eight years ago when she let her father and her godmother, Lady Russell, persuade her to break off an engagement to Frederic Wentworth because he was a naval officer heading into war and his family had no money. Anne didn't care about money and she was willing to take her chances with war, but her desire to please her family won out and she decided not to marry the only man she ever loved. Lady Russell assured her that in time she'd be glad she didn't marry Frederic, but it seems Lady Russell was wrong.

Eight years after breaking his heart, Anne comes face to face with Frederic again. Now, he is wealthy and her family's fortune has dwindled considerably. She would like to tell him that she is older and wiser now, but she can barely utter a hello when she sees him. Besides, with so many young women vying for his affection, she can't expect him to give her a second chance. Can she? Could he be persuaded?

What Makes Anne Elliot So Memorable?

Anne Elliot is memorable for anyone who has ever suffered from heartache—and for those who have longed for or been granted a second chance. And, of course, she is unforgettable to anyone who was ever young and in love. For anyone else, Anne may seem like a plain and dull woman in an otherwise charismatic family.

The Life and Times of Jane Austen

Jane Austen, born in 1775, was part of a close-knit family. Based on journal entries, she seemed to have a happy childhood and preferred the company of her family to that of others. Her father and her brother James invested a lot of their time in Austen's education. She let them know early on that she wanted to be a novelist and—foregoing marriage—devoted her life to writing. Between 1811 and 1816, she wrote *Sense and Sensibility*, *Pride and Prejudice*, *Mansfield Park*, and *Emma*. Since she published her work anonymously, Austen was not famous in her lifetime. Her books were also overshadowed by the hugely popular Charles Dickens, and not taken as seriously as George Eliot's. *Persuasion* and *Northanger Abby* were Austen's last completed works, but neither novel was published until after her death at age forty-one in 1817. In 1869, her nephew, an aspiring novelist, wrote a book titled *A Memoir of Jane Austen* that sparked a newfound interest in her work among scholars and everyday readers alike.

FROM *Persuasion*

Vanity was the beginning and the end of Sir Walter Elliot's character; vanity of person and of situation. He had been remarkably handsome in his youth; and, at fifty-four was still a very fine man. Few women could think more of their personal appearance than he did, nor could the valet of any new made lord be more delighted with the place he held in society. He considered the blessing of beauty as inferior only to the blessing of a baronetcy; and the Sir Walter Elliot, who united these gifts, was the constant object of his warmest respect and devotion.

Novel Knowledge: JANE AUSTEN'S DEATH

The notion that Jane Austen died of Addison's disease, a rare illness that affects the body's production of hormones, has come under scrutiny. Some who live with the disease claim she could have never dictated a poem to her sister two days before her death if she truly died of Addison's. Some scholars speculate that she may have died from lymphoma. Others believe it is more likely she contracted tuberculosis, a common cause of death during that time.

His good looks and his rank had one fair claim on his attachment; since to them he must have owed a wife of very superior character to anything deserved by his own. Lady Elliot had been an excellent woman, sensible and amiable; whose judgement and conduct, if they might be pardoned the youthful infatuation which made her Lady Elliot, had never required indulgence afterwards.—She had humoured, or softened, or concealed his failings, and promoted his real respectability for seventeen years; and though not the very happiest being in the world herself, had found enough in her duties, her friends, and her children, to attach her to life, and make it no matter of indifference to her when she was called on to quit them.—Three girls, the two eldest sixteen and fourteen, was an awful legacy for a mother to bequeath, an awful charge rather, to confide to the authority and guidance of a conceited, silly father. She had, however, one very intimate friend, a sensible, deserving woman, who had been brought, by strong attachment to herself, to settle close by her, in the village of Kellynch; and on her kindness and advice, Lady Elliot mainly relied for the best help and maintenance of the good principles and instruction which she had been anxiously giving her daughters.

This friend, and Sir Walter, did not marry, whatever might have been anticipated on that head by their acquaintance. Thirteen years had passed away since Lady Elliot's death, and they were still near neighbours and intimate friends, and one remained a widower, the other a widow.

That Lady Russell, of steady age and character, and extremely well provided for, should have no thought of a second marriage, needs no apology to the public, which is rather apt to be unreasonably discontented when a woman does marry again, than when she does not; but Sir Walter's continuing in singleness requires explanation. Be it known then, that Sir Walter, like a good father, (having met with one or two private disappointments in very unreasonable applications), prided himself on remaining single for his dear daughters' sake. For one daughter, his eldest, he would really have given up any thing, which he had not been very much tempted to do. Elizabeth had succeeded, at sixteen, to all that was possible, of her mother's rights and consequence; and being very handsome, and very like himself, her influence had always been great, and they had gone on together most happily. His two other children were of very inferior value. Mary had acquired a little artificial importance, by becoming Mrs Charles Musgrove; but Anne, with an elegance of mind and sweetness of character, which must have placed her high with any people of real understanding, was nobody with either father or sister; her word had no weight, her convenience was always to give way—she was only Anne.

Close your eyes for the next five minutes and imagine Jesus sitting beside you. Take His hand. Open your heart. By what name does your heart welcome him? What do you want to share with him at this time?

To Lady Russell, indeed, she was a most dear and highly valued god-daughter, favourite, and friend. Lady Russell loved them all; but it was only in Anne that she could fancy the mother to revive again.

A few years before, Anne Elliot had been a very pretty girl, but her bloom had vanished early; and as even in its height, her father had found little to admire in her, (so totally different were her delicate features and mild dark eyes from his own), there could be nothing in them, now that she was faded and thin, to excite his esteem. He had never indulged much hope, he had now none, of ever reading her name in any other page of his favourite work. All equality of alliance must rest with Elizabeth, for Mary had merely connected herself with an old country family of respectability and large fortune, and had therefore given all the honour and received none: Elizabeth would, one day or other, marry suitably.

It sometimes happens that a woman is handsomer at twenty-nine than she was ten years before; and, generally speaking, if there has been neither ill health nor anxiety, it is a time of life at which scarcely any charm is lost. It was so with Elizabeth, still the same handsome Miss Elliot that she had begun to be thirteen years ago, and Sir Walter might be excused, therefore, in forgetting her age, or, at least, be deemed only half a fool, for thinking himself and Elizabeth as blooming as ever, amidst the wreck of the good looks of everybody else; for he could plainly see how old all the rest of his family and acquaintance were growing. Anne haggard, Mary coarse, every face in the neighbourhood worsting, and the rapid increase of the crow's foot about Lady Russell's temples had long been a distress to him.

Elizabeth did not quite equal her father in personal contentment. Thirteen years had seen her mistress of Kellynch Hall, presiding and directing with a self-possession and decision which could never have given the idea of her being younger than she was. For thirteen years had she been doing the honours, and laying down the domestic law at home, and leading the way to the chaise and four, and walking immediately after Lady Russell out of all the drawing-rooms and dining-rooms in the country. Thirteen winters' revolving frosts had seen her opening every ball of credit which a scanty neighbourhood afforded, and thirteen springs shewn their blossoms, as she travelled up to London with her father, for a few weeks' annual enjoyment of the great world. She had the remembrance of all this, she had the consciousness of being nine-and-twenty to give her some regrets and some apprehensions; she was fully satisfied of being still quite as handsome as ever, but she felt her approach to the years of danger, and would have rejoiced to be certain of being properly solicited by baronet-blood within the next twelvemonth or two. Then might she again take up the book of books with as much enjoyment as in her early youth, but now she liked it not. Always to be presented with the date of her own birth and see no marriage follow but that of a youngest sister, made the book an evil; and more than once, when her father had left it open on the table near her, had she closed it, with averted eyes, and pushed it away.

She had had a disappointment, moreover, which that book, and especially the history of her own family, must ever present the remembrance of. The heir presumptive, the very William Walter Elliot, Esq., whose rights had been so generously supported by her father, had disappointed her.

She had, while a very young girl, as soon as she had known him to be, in the event of her having no brother, the future baronet, meant to marry him, and her father had always meant that she should. He had not been known to them as a boy; but soon after Lady Elliot's death, Sir Walter had sought the acquaintance, and though his overtures had not been met with any warmth, he had persevered in seeking it, making allowance for the modest drawing-back of youth; and, in one of their spring excursions to London, when Elizabeth was in her first bloom, Mr Elliot had been forced into the introduction.

He was at that time a very young man, just engaged in the study of the law; and Elizabeth found him extremely agreeable, and every plan in his favour was confirmed. He was invited to Kellynch Hall; he was talked of and expected all the rest of the year; but he never came. The following spring he was seen again in town, found equally agreeable, again encouraged, invited, and expected, and again he did not come; and the next tidings were that he was married. Instead of pushing his fortune in the line marked out for the heir of the house of Elliot, he had purchased independence by uniting himself to a rich woman of inferior birth.

Sir Walter has resented it. As the head of the house, he felt that he ought to have been consulted, especially after taking the young man so publicly by the hand; "For they must have been seen together," he observed, "once at Tattersall's, and twice in the lobby of the House of Commons." His disapprobation was expressed, but apparently very little regarded. Mr Elliot had attempted no apology, and shewn himself as unsolicitous of being longer noticed by the family, as Sir Walter considered him unworthy of it: all acquaintance between them had ceased.

This very awkward history of Mr Elliot was still, after an interval of several years, felt with anger by Elizabeth, who had liked the man for himself, and still more for being her father's heir, and whose strong family pride could see only in him a proper match for Sir Walter Elliot's eldest daughter. There was not a baronet from A to Z whom her feelings could have so willingly acknowledged as an equal. Yet so miserably had he conducted himself, that though she was at this present time (the summer of 1814) wearing black ribbons for his wife, she could not admit him to be worth thinking of again. The disgrace of his first marriage might, perhaps, as there was no reason to suppose it perpetuated by offspring, have been got over, had he not done worse; but he had, as by the accustomary intervention of kind friends, they had been informed, spoken most disrespectfully of them all, most slightingly and contemptuously of the very blood he belonged to, and the honours which were hereafter to be his own. This could not be pardoned.

Novel Knowledge: A FAN OF THE NAVY

In *Persuasion,* high society types like Anne's father, Sir William Elliot, turn up their noses at navy men. The naval officers, however, prove to be the finest men in the novel. Jane Austen's brothers Francis and Charles—both naval officers whom she adored—most likely inspired her.

Such were Elizabeth Elliot's sentiments and sensations; such the cares to alloy, the agitations to vary, the sameness and the elegance, the prosperity and the nothingness of her scene of life; such the feelings to give interest to a long, uneventful residence in one country circle, to fill the vacancies which there were no habits of utility abroad, no talents or accomplishments for home, to occupy.

But now, another occupation and solicitude of mind was beginning to be added to these. Her father was growing distressed for money. She knew, that when he now took up the Baronetage, it was to drive the heavy bills of his tradespeople, and the unwelcome hints of Mr Shepherd, his agent, from his thoughts. The Kellynch property was good, but not equal to Sir Walter's apprehension of the state required in its possessor. While Lady Elliot lived, there had been method, moderation, and economy, which had just kept him within his income; but with her had died all such right-mindedness, and from that period he had been constantly exceeding it. It had not been possible for him to spend less; he had done nothing but what Sir Walter Elliot was imperiously called on to do; but blameless as he was, he was not only growing dreadfully in debt, but was hearing of it so often, that it became vain to attempt concealing it longer, even partially, from his daughter. He had given her some hints of it the last spring in town; he had gone so far even as to say, "Can we retrench? Does it occur to you that there is any one article in which we can retrench?" and Elizabeth, to do her justice, had, in the first ardour of female alarm, set seriously to think what could be done, and had finally proposed these two branches of economy, to cut off some unnecessary charities, and to refrain from new furnishing the drawing-room; to which expedients she afterwards added the happy thought of their taking no present down to Anne, as had been the usual yearly custom. But these measures, however good in themselves, were insufficient for the real extent of the evil, the whole of which Sir Walter found himself obliged to confess to her soon afterwards. Elizabeth had nothing to propose of deeper efficacy. She felt herself ill-used and unfortunate, as did her father; and they were neither of them able to devise any means of lessening their expenses without compromising their dignity, or relinquishing their comforts in a way not to be borne.

Jane Eyre

IN *JANE EYRE* BY CHARLOTTE BRONTË
FIRST PUBLISHED IN: 1847

Who is she? A soft-spoken woman who lets no one take her for granted.

Her Story

Orphaned as a child, Jane Eyre learns early on that nothing worth having is going to come easy. First, she is forced to live with an abusive aunt. Then, she is sent to Lowood, a school for troubled—or, in Jane's case, unwanted—girls. The school is harsh, but Jane manages to make friends and even find a mentor. By the time she leaves Lowood, Jane is well-schooled and wise beyond her years. Searching for a way to start a life of her own, she takes a job as the governess to Edward Rochester's little girl.

Though Jane, plain-faced and reserved, looks like a simple woman, Edward quickly comes to realize that she is like no woman he has ever met. She has a complex, old soul and her mere presence demands respect. She is quick to respond to his criticism with a soft, but stern tone—something Edward is not accustomed to hearing. She gets right to the heart of matters and he is better for it.

An attraction forms between the two. Over time, the attraction turns to mutual love and respect. Edward wants Jane to be his wife, but loving Edward is not easy. An ugly past weighs on him, and Jane must decide if a life with Edward Rochester is really a life she wants.

What Makes Jane Eyre So Memorable?

While women in fiction often make their mark with shocking, rebellious behavior, Jane Eyre is just the opposite. Her nature is soft and careful, but she's hardly anyone's fool. She is a strong, smart woman with opinions and a virtuous streak—a rarely portrayed combination of traits. However, these traits do not make her the judgmental type one might expect. She has better things to do with her time.

The Life and Times of Charlotte Brontë

Born in 1816, in Yorkshire, England, Charlotte Brontë was the daughter of a clergyman, but like her sisters, Anne and Emily, Charlotte aspired to be a novelist. After a stint at Clergy Daughter's School in Lancashire with her sister Emily from 1824 to 1825, Charlotte went to Brussels to learn French and German.

When she returned, Charlotte became a teacher and a governess, but during this time period she was quietly writing her first novel, *Jane Eyre*. After the novel's publication and huge success, she quit her job and devoted all of her time to writing. In June 1854, she married Arthur Bell Nicholls, and soon after the wedding, she became pregnant. Unfortunately, complications during her pregnancy proved fatal. Charlotte was only thirty-eight years old when she died.

From *Jane Eyre*

Two wax candles stood lighted on the table, and two on the mantelpiece; basking in the light and heat of a superb fire, lay Pilot—Adèle knelt near him. Half reclined on a couch appeared Mr. Rochester, his foot supported by the cushion; he was looking at Adèle and the dog: the fire shone full on his face. I knew my traveller with his broad and jetty eyebrows; his square forehead, made squarer by the horizontal sweep of his black hair. I recognised his decisive nose, more remarkable for character than beauty; his full nostrils, denoting, I thought, choler; his grim mouth, chin, and jaw—yes, all three were very grim, and no mistake. His shape, now divested of cloak, I perceived harmonised in squareness with his physiognomy: I suppose it was a good figure in the athletic sense of the term—broad chested and thin flanked, though neither tall nor graceful.

Mr. Rochester must have been aware of the entrance of Mrs. Fairfax and myself; but it appeared he was not in the mood to notice us, for he never lifted his head as we approached.

"Here is Miss Eyre, sir," said Mrs. Fairfax, in her quiet way. He bowed, still not taking his eyes from the group of the dog and child.

Novel Knowledge: FALLING FOR AN OLDER MAN

While studying in Brussels, Charlotte Brontë fell in love with her teacher, Monsieur Heger, who was married and had a family. He was most likely the inspiration for the character of Edward Rochester. However, Heger did not show the same attraction for Charlotte that Rochester showed for Jane, and Charlotte left Brussels quietly heartbroken.

"Let Miss Eyre be seated," said he: and there was something in the forced stiff bow, in the impatient yet formal tone, which seemed further to express, "What the deuce is it to me whether Miss Eyre be there or not? At this moment I am not disposed to accost her."

I sat down quite disembarrassed. A reception of finished politeness would probably have confused me: I could not have returned or repaid it by answering grace and elegance on my part; but harsh caprice laid me under no obligation; on the contrary, a decent quiescence, under the freak of manner, gave me the advantage. Besides, the eccentricity of the proceeding was piquant: I felt interested to see how he would go on.

He went on as a statue would, that is, he neither spoke nor moved. Mrs. Fairfax seemed to think it necessary that some one should be amiable, and she began to talk. Kindly, as usual—and, as usual, rather trite—she condoled with him on the pressure of business he had had all day; on the annoyance it must have been to him with that painful sprain: then she commended his patience and perseverance in going through with it.

"Madam, I should like some tea," was the sole rejoinder she got. She hastened to ring the bell; and when the tray came, she proceeded to arrange the cups, spoons, &c., with assiduous celerity. I and Adèle went to the table; but the master did not leave his couch.

"Will you hand Mr. Rochester's cup?" said Mrs. Fairfax to me; "Adèle might perhaps spill it."

I did as requested. As he took the cup from my hand, Adèle, thinking the moment propitious for making a request in my favour, cried out—

"N'est-ce pas, monsieur, qu'il y a un cadeau pour Mademoiselle Eyre dans votre petit coffre?"

"Who talks of cadeaux?" said he gruffly. "Did you expect a present, Miss Eyre? Are you fond of presents?" and he searched my face with eyes that I saw were dark, irate, and piercing.

"I hardly know, sir; I have little experience of them: they are generally thought pleasant things."

"Generally thought? But what do you think?"

"I should be obliged to take time, sir, before I could give you an answer worthy of your acceptance: a present has many faces to it, has it not? and one should consider all, before pronouncing an opinion as to its nature."

"Miss Eyre, you are not so unsophisticated as Adèle: she demands a 'cadeau,' clamorously, the moment she sees me: you beat about the bush."

"Because I have less confidence in my deserts than Adèle has: she can prefer the claim of old acquaintance, and the right too of custom; for she says you have always been in the habit of giving her playthings; but if I had to make out a case I should be puzzled, since I am a stranger, and have done nothing to entitle me to an acknowledgment."

"Oh, don't fall back on over-modesty! I have examined Adèle, and find you have taken great pains with her: she is not bright, she has no talents; yet in a short time she has made much improvement."

"Sir, you have now given me my 'cadeau;' I am obliged to you: it is the meed teachers most covet—praise of their pupils' progress."

"Humph!" said Mr. Rochester, and he took his tea in silence.

"Come to the fire," said the master, when the tray was taken away, and Mrs. Fairfax had settled into a corner with her knitting; while Adèle was leading me by the hand round the room, showing me the beautiful books and ornaments on the consoles and chiffonnières. We obeyed, as in duty bound; Adèle wanted to take a seat on my knee, but she was ordered to amuse herself with Pilot.

"You have been resident in my house three months?"

"Yes, sir."

"And you came from—?"

"From Lowood school, in —shire."

"Ah! a charitable concern. How long were you there?"

"Eight years."

"Eight years! you must be tenacious of life. I thought half the time in such a place would have done up any constitution! No wonder you have rather the look of another world. I marvelled where you had got that sort of face. When you came on me in Hay Lane last night, I thought unaccountably of fairy tales, and had half a mind to demand whether you had bewitched my horse: I am not sure yet. Who are your parents?"

"I have none."

"Nor ever had, I suppose: do you remember them?"

"No."

"I thought not. And so you were waiting for your people when you sat on that stile?"

"For whom, sir?"

"For the men in green: it was a proper moonlight evening for them. Did I break through one of your rings, that you spread that damned ice on the causeway?"

I shook my head. "The men in green all forsook England a hundred years ago," said I, speaking as seriously as he had done. "And not even in Hay Lane, or the fields about it, could you find a trace of them. I don't think either summer or harvest, or winter moon, will ever shine on their revels more."

Mrs. Fairfax had dropped her knitting, and, with raised eyebrows, seemed wondering what sort of talk this was.

"Well," resumed Mr. Rochester, "if you disown parents, you must have some sort of kinsfolk: uncles and aunts?"

"No; none that I ever saw."

"And your home?"

"I have none."

"Where do your brothers and sisters live?"

"I have no brothers or sisters."

"Who recommended you to come here?"

"I advertised, and Mrs. Fairfax answered my advertisement."

"Yes," said the good lady, who now knew what ground we were upon, "and I am daily thankful for the choice Providence led me to make. Miss Eyre has been an invaluable companion to me, and a kind and careful teacher to Adèle."

"Don't trouble yourself to give her a character," returned Mr. Rochester: "eulogiums will not bias me; I shall judge for myself. She began by felling my horse."

"Sir?" said Mrs. Fairfax.

"I have to thank her for this sprain."

The widow looked bewildered.

"Miss Eyre, have you ever lived in a town?"

"No, sir."

"Have you seen much society?"

"None but the pupils and teachers of Lowood, and now the inmates of Thornfield."

"Have you read much?"

"Only such books as came in my way; and they have not been numerous or very learned."

"You have lived the life of a nun: no doubt you are well drilled in religious forms;—Brocklehurst, who I understand directs Lowood, is a parson, is he not?"

"Yes, sir."

"And you girls probably worshipped him, as a convent full of religieuses would worship their director."

"Oh, no."

"You are very cool! No! What! a novice not worship her priest! That sounds blasphemous."

"I disliked Mr. Brocklehurst; and I was not alone in the feeling. He is a harsh man; at once pompous and meddling; he cut off our hair; and for economy's sake bought us bad needles and thread, with which we could hardly sew."

"That was very false economy," remarked Mrs. Fairfax, who now again caught the drift of the dialogue.

"And was that the head and front of his offending?" demanded Mr. Rochester.

"He starved us when he had the sole superintendence of the pro-vision department, before the committee was appointed; and he bored us with long lectures once a week, and with evening read-ings from books of his own inditing, about sudden deaths and judgments, which made us afraid to go to bed."

"What age were you when you went to Lowood?"

"About ten."

"And you stayed there eight years: you are now, then, eighteen?"

I assented.

"Arithmetic, you see, is useful; without its aid, I should hardly have been able to guess your age. It is a point difficult to fix where the features and countenance are so much at variance as in your case. And now what did you learn at Lowood? Can you play?"

"A little."

"Of course: that is the established answer. Go into the library—I mean, if you please.—(Excuse my tone of command; I am used to say, 'Do this,' and it is done: I cannot alter my customary habits for one new inmate.)—Go, then, into the library; take a candle with you; leave the door open; sit down to the piano, and play a tune."

I departed, obeying his directions.

"Enough!" he called out in a few minutes. "You play a little, I see; like any other English school-girl; perhaps rather better than some, but not well."

I closed the piano and returned. Mr. Rochester continued— "Adèle showed me some sketches this morning, which she said were yours. I don't know whether they were entirely of your doing; probably a master aided you?"

"No, indeed!" I interjected.

"Ah! that pricks pride. Well, fetch me your portfolio, if you can vouch for its contents being original; but don't pass your word unless you are certain: I can recognise patchwork."

"Then I will say nothing, and you shall judge for yourself, sir."

I brought the portfolio from the library.

"Approach the table," said he; and I wheeled it to his couch. Adèle and Mrs. Fairfax drew near to see the pictures.

"No crowding," said Mr. Rochester: "take the drawings from my hand as I finish with them; but don't push your faces up to mine."

He deliberately scrutinised each sketch and painting. Three he laid aside; the others, when he had examined them, he swept from him.

"Take them off to the other table, Mrs. Fairfax," said he, "and look at them with Adèle;—you" (glancing at me) "resume your seat, and answer my questions. I perceive those pictures were done by one hand: was that hand yours?"

"Yes."

"And when did you find time to do them? They have taken much time, and some thought."

"I did them in the last two vacations I spent at Lowood, when I had no other occupation."

"Where did you get your copies?"

"Out of my head."

"That head I see now on your shoulders?"

"Yes, sir."

"Has it other furniture of the same kind within?"

"I should think it may have: I should hope—better."

He spread the pictures before him, and again surveyed them alternately.

. . . "Were you happy when you painted these pictures?" asked Mr. Rochester presently.

"I was absorbed, sir: yes, and I was happy. To paint them, in short, was to enjoy one of the keenest pleasures I have ever known."

"That is not saying much. Your pleasures, by your own account, have been few; but I daresay you did exist in a kind of artist's dreamland while you blent and arranged these strange tints. Did you sit at them long each day?"

"I had nothing else to do, because it was the vacation, and I sat at them from morning till noon, and from noon till night: the length of the midsummer days favoured my inclination to apply."

"And you felt self-satisfied with the result of your ardent labours?"

"Far from it. I was tormented by the contrast between my idea and my handiwork: in each case I had imagined something which I was quite powerless to realise."

"Not quite: you have secured the shadow of your thought; but no more, probably. You had not enough of the artist's skill and science to give it full being: yet the drawings are, for a school-girl, peculiar. As to the thoughts, they are elfish. These eyes in the Evening Star you must have seen in a dream. How could you make them look so clear, and yet not at all brilliant? for the planet above quells their rays. And what meaning is that in their solemn depth? And who taught you to paint wind? There is a high gale in that sky, and on this hill-top. Where did you see Latmos? For that is Latmos. There! put the drawings away!"

Novel Knowledge: THREE SISTERS, TWO COPIES

In 1846, Charlotte, Emily, and Anne Brontë published a collection of poetry together under the pen names of Currer, Ellis, and Acton Bell. Only two copies of the book were ever sold.

I had scarce tied the strings of the portfolio, when, looking at his watch, he said abruptly—

"It is nine o'clock: what are you about, Miss Eyre, to let Adèle sit up so long? Take her to bed."

Adèle went to kiss him before quitting the room: he endured the caress, but scarcely seemed to relish it more than Pilot would have done, nor so much.

"I wish you all good-night, now," said he, making a movement of the hand towards the door, in token that he was tired of our company, and wished to dismiss us. Mrs. Fairfax folded up her knitting: I took my portfolio: we curtseyed to him, received a frigid bow in return, and so withdrew.

Catherine Earnshaw

IN *WUTHERING HEIGHTS* BY EMILY BRONTË
FIRST PUBLISHED IN: 1847

Who is she? A passionate woman torn between the life of a refined lady and that of a wild, savage girl still in love with her childhood friend.

Her Story

Catherine Earnshaw hates to wear shoes or eat slowly. She laughs if something is funny to her, even if it might offend others, and she can't seem to walk—she must always run. In short, she is as untamed and beautiful as the land she has grown up in—the Moors.

Novel Knowledge: A SISTER'S EDITS

Though *Wuthering Heights* was first published in 1847 in three volumes, Charlotte Brontë took it upon herself to edit the story and publish it again in 1850 under Emily's name.

When Mr. Earnshaw, her good-natured father, brings an orphaned boy named Heathcliff home, Catherine's brother, Hindley, explodes with jealousy, but Catherine finds a friend. The two are kindred and wild spirits. Together they have no use for anything or anyone else; they are happy in their secluded world. But when Mr. Earnshaw dies unexpectedly everything changes. Hindley takes over as the rightful heir to the family estate and treats Heathcliff as if he were a servant—or worse. Catherine tries to defend Heathcliff, but she has no influence over her brother.

Nelly, the woman who has looked after Catherine since her mother died, begins encouraging her to act like a lady (at least wear shoes) and show some manners (at least at the table). At first, Catherine ignores Nelly's suggestions, but over time she begins to realize that her future lies in the hands of the man she marries. Perhaps she should do as Nelly says. She knows that a wealthy young man named Linton would like to marry her, but no matter how hard she tries to change, her heart still belongs to Heathcliff—a man with nothing.

Heathcliff asks Catherine to run away with him, but when she merely hesitates he packs his bags and leaves bitter and broken hearted before she has the chance to say yes. She waits three years for him to return before she gives up and marries Linton. When Heathcliff finally does return, Catherine refuses to suffer quietly for the sake of others, not even for her good and patient husband; she makes her feelings known to all. She still loves Heathcliff, but now hates him with a passion that is just as strong. She cannot forgive him for abandoning her, but she finds that she cannot live in peace without him.

What Makes Catherine Earnshaw So Memorable?

As a little girl Catherine is pretty in her bare feet, easily forgiven for her inappropriate outbursts of laughter, and only occasionally scolded for her hot temper. She loves animals and nature, but she is insensitive, sometimes even cruel to people. As a woman her bad behavior is frowned upon and she knows everyone expects her to change. The only problem is that Catherine doesn't really want to change. She only wants what she wants and to hell with everything—and everyone—else.

Today, over a century after Brontë created her, Catherine is still an original and difficult character for readers to fully grasp. She is violent, bitter, and selfish, but her love for Heathcliff softens our hearts even as it hardens her own.

The Life and Times of Emily Brontë

Wuthering Heights is the only novel Emily Brontë wrote. Born in 1818, in Thornton, England, her father moved the family to Haworth, an isolated rural village in West Yorkshire, England. Her mother died when she was three, so her sisters helped raise her. She grew up reading Shakespeare, Milton, and the Bible and, like her sisters, found writing to be a wonderful source of creativity and entertainment. Based on her early poems, some believe that Emily was the most opinionated and independent of the three sisters, but it's hard to know. She and her sister Charlotte planned for many years to open a school for girls, but they never saw this dream to fruition. Emily Brontë never married and, like all the Brontë sisters, she didn't live to see old age. In 1848, she died of tuberculosis. She was only twenty-nine.

FROM *Wuthering Heights*

Certainly she had ways with her such as I never saw a child take up before; and she put all of us past our patience fifty times and oftener in a day: from the hour she came down-stairs till the hour she went to bed, we had not a minute's security that she wouldn't be in mischief. Her spirits were always at high-water mark, her tongue always going—singing, laughing, and plaguing everybody who would not do the same. A wild, wicked slip she was—but she had the bonniest eye, the sweetest smile, and lightest foot in the parish: and, after all, I believe she meant no harm; for when once she made you cry in good earnest, it seldom happened that she would not keep you company, and oblige you to be quiet that you might comfort her. She was much too fond of Heathcliff. The greatest punishment we could invent for her was to keep her separate from him: yet she got chided more than any of us on his account. In play, she liked exceedingly to act the little mistress; using her hands freely, and commanding her companions: she did so to me, but I would not bear slapping and ordering; and so I let her know.

Now, Mr. Earnshaw did not understand jokes from his children: he had always been strict and grave with them; and Catherine, on her part, had no idea why her father should be crosser and less patient in his ailing condition than he was in his prime. His peevish reproofs wakened in her a naughty delight to provoke him: she was never so happy as when we were all scolding her at once, and she defying us with her bold, saucy look, and her ready words; turning Joseph's religious curses into ridicule, baiting me, and doing just what her father hated most—showing how her pretended insolence, which he thought real, had more power over Heathcliff than his kindness: how the boy would do her bidding in anything, and his only when it suited his own inclination. After behaving as badly as possible all day, she sometimes came fondling to make it up at night. 'Nay, Cathy,' the old man would say, 'I cannot love thee, thou'rt worse than thy brother. Go, say thy prayers, child, and ask God's pardon. I doubt thy mother and I must rue that we ever reared thee!' That made her cry, at first; and then being repulsed continually hardened her, and she laughed if I told her to say she was sorry for her faults, and beg to be forgiven.

But the hour came, at last, that ended Mr. Earnshaw's troubles on earth. He died quietly in his chair one October evening, seated by the fire-side. A high wind blustered round the house, and roared in the chimney: it sounded wild and stormy, yet it was not cold, and we were all together—I, a little removed from the hearth, busy at my knitting, and Joseph reading his Bible near the table (for the servants generally sat in the house then, after their work was done). Miss Cathy had been sick, and that made her still;

she leant against her father's knee, and Heathcliff was lying on the floor with his head in her lap. I remember the master, before he fell into a doze, stroking her bonny hair—it pleased him rarely to see her gentle—and saying, 'Why canst thou not always be a good lass, Cathy?' And she turned her face up to his, and laughed, and answered, 'Why cannot you always be a good man, father?' But as soon as she saw him vexed again, she kissed his hand, and said she would sing him to sleep. She began singing very low, till his fingers dropped from hers, and his head sank on his breast. Then I told her to hush, and not stir, for fear she should wake him. We all kept as mute as mice a full half-hour, and should have done so longer, only Joseph, having finished his chapter, got up and said that he must rouse the master for prayers and bed. He stepped forward, and called him by name, and touched his shoulder; but he would not move: so he took the candle and looked at him. I thought there was something wrong as he set down the light; and seizing the children each by an arm, whispered them to 'frame up-stairs, and make little din—they might pray alone that evening—he had summut to do.'

'I shall bid father good-night first,' said Catherine, putting her arms round his neck, before we could hinder her. The poor thing discovered her loss directly—she screamed out—'Oh, he's dead, Heathcliff! he's dead!' And they both set up a heart-breaking cry.

I joined my wail to theirs, loud and bitter; but Joseph asked what we could be thinking of to roar in that way over a saint in heaven. He told me to put on my cloak and run to Gimmerton for the doctor and the parson. I could not guess the use that either would be of, then. However, I went, through wind and rain, and brought one, the doctor, back with me; the other said he would come in the morning. Leaving Joseph to explain matters, I ran to the children's room: their door was ajar, I saw they had never lain down, though it was past midnight; but they were calmer, and did not need me to console them. The little souls were comforting each other with better thoughts than I could have hit on: no parson in the world ever pictured heaven so beautifully as they did, in their innocent talk; and, while I sobbed and listened, I could not help wishing we were all there safe together.

* * * *

I was superstitious about dreams then, and am still; and Catherine had an unusual gloom in her aspect, that made me dread something from which I might shape a prophecy, and foresee a fearful catastrophe. She was vexed, but she did not proceed. Apparently taking up another subject, she recommenced in a short time.

Novel Knowledge: A HOMEBODY

Emily was so fond of her life at home that she only lasted six months as a governess before quitting. She returned to her own home claiming she missed her family too much to stay away.

'If I were in heaven, Nelly, I should be extremely miserable.'

'Because you are not fit to go there,' I answered. 'All sinners would be miserable in heaven.'

'But it is not for that. I dreamt once that I was there.'

'I tell you I won't hearken to your dreams, Miss Catherine! I'll go to bed,' I interrupted again.

She laughed, and held me down; for I made a motion to leave my chair.

'This is nothing,' cried she: 'I was only going to say that heaven did not seem to be my home; and I broke my heart with weeping to come back to earth; and the angels were so angry that they flung me out into the middle of the heath on the top of Wuthering Heights; where I woke sobbing for joy. That will do to explain my secret, as well as the other. I've no more business to marry Edgar Linton than I have to be in heaven; and if the wicked man in there had not brought Heathcliff so low, I shouldn't have thought of it. It would degrade me to marry Heathcliff now; so he shall never know how I love him: and that, not because he's handsome, Nelly, but because he's more myself than I am. Whatever our souls are made of, his and mine are the same; and Linton's is as different as a moonbeam from lightning, or frost from fire.'

Ere this speech ended I became sensible of Heathcliff's presence. Having noticed a slight movement, I turned my head, and saw him rise from the bench, and steal out noiselessly. He had listened till he heard Catherine say it would degrade her to marry him, and then he stayed to hear no further. My companion, sitting on the ground, was prevented by the back of the settle from remarking his presence or departure; but I started, and bade her hush!

'Why?' she asked, gazing nervously round.

'Joseph is here,' I answered, catching opportunely the roll of his cartwheels up the road; 'and Heathcliff will come in with him. I'm not sure whether he were not at the door this moment.'

'Oh, he couldn't overhear me at the door!' said she. 'Give me Hareton, while you get the supper, and when it is ready ask me to sup with you. I want to cheat my uncomfortable conscience, and be convinced that Heathcliff has no notion of these things. He has not, has he? He does not know what being in love is!'

'I see no reason that he should not know, as well as you,' I returned; 'and if you are his choice, he'll be the most unfortunate creature that ever was born! As soon as you become Mrs. Linton, he loses friend, and love, and all! Have you considered how you'll bear the separation, and how he'll bear to be quite deserted in the world? Because, Miss Catherine—'

'He quite deserted! we separated!' she exclaimed, with an accent of indignation. 'Who is to separate us, pray? They'll meet the fate of Milo! Not as long as I live, Ellen: for no mortal creature. Every Linton on the face of the earth might melt into nothing before I could consent to forsake Heathcliff. Oh, that's not what I intend—that's not what I mean! I shouldn't be Mrs. Linton were such a price demanded! He'll be as much to me as he has been all his lifetime. Edgar must shake off his antipathy, and tolerate him, at least. He will, when he learns my true feelings towards him. Nelly, I see now you think me a selfish wretch; but did it never strike you that if Heathcliff and I married, we should be beggars? whereas, if I marry Linton I can aid Heathcliff to rise, and place him out of my brother's power.'

'With your husband's money, Miss Catherine?' I asked. 'You'll find him not so pliable as you calculate upon: and, though I'm hardly a judge, I think that's the worst motive you've given yet for being the wife of young Linton.'

'It is not,' retorted she; 'it is the best! The others were the satisfaction of my whims: and for Edgar's sake, too, to satisfy him. This is for the sake of one who comprehends in his person my feelings to Edgar and myself. I cannot express it; but surely you and everybody have a notion that there is or should be an existence of yours beyond you. What were the use of my creation, if I were entirely contained here? My great miseries in this world have been Heathcliff's miseries, and I watched and felt each from the beginning: my great thought in living is himself. If all else perished, and he remained, I should still continue to be; and if all else remained, and he were annihilated, the universe would turn to a mighty stranger: I should not seem a part of it.—My love for Linton is like the foliage in the woods: time will change it, I'm well aware, as winter changes the trees. My love for Heathcliff resembles the eternal rocks beneath: a source of little visible delight, but necessary. Nelly, I am Heathcliff! He's always, always in my mind: not as a pleasure, any more than I am always a pleasure to myself, but as my own being. So don't talk of our separation again: it is impracticable; and—'

She paused, and hid her face in the folds of my gown; but I jerked it forcibly away. I was out of patience with her folly!

Holly Golightly

IN *BREAKFAST AT TIFFANY'S* BY TRUMAN CAPOTE
FIRST PUBLISHED IN: 1958

Who is she? A glamorous girl searching for a place to call home.

Her Story

Holiday "Holly" Golightly loves men—older, wealthy men. She also loves New York, or at least she says she does. She will do marijuana on occasion, but prefers bourbon. She stays out all night, and she keeps a cat she never names. We learn about Holly through an unnamed narrator who lives in the same apartment building. He's an aspiring writer who is admittedly smitten with Holly and pays close attention to the details of her life.

Holly confides to her neighbor that she sometimes gets what she calls "the mean reds"—a feeling she has that something horrible is going to happen, even though she can't imagine what it could be. Her solution? "What I've found does the most good is just to get into a taxi and go to Tiffany's. It calms me down right away, the quietness and the proud look of it; nothing very bad could happen to you there, not with those kind men in their nice suits, and that lovely smell of silver and alligator wallets. If I could find a real-life place that makes me feel like Tiffany's, then I'd buy some furniture, and give the cat a name."

Holly is from Texas, but she doesn't want anyone to know that or much of anything else about her past. She lives in the moment doing exactly as she pleases—unless she's busy dreaming about her future that is. Unfortunately her high-flying, carefree lifestyle gets her into a lot of trouble and on the front page of all the New York papers.

What Makes Holly Golightly So Memorable?

Everything about Holly Golightly is exciting and over the top, but a little sad. She's hard to know and impossible to forget. By her own admission she has a lot of gall. She has style, if not always good taste, and she likes to tell just enough about herself to keep people interested and guessing. Why else would she say things like, "Of course people couldn't help but think I must be a bit of a dyke myself. And of course I am. Everyone is: a bit. So what? That never discouraged a man yet, in fact it seems to goad them on."

We are never sure if what Holly is saying is true or not, but we don't really care. She's fun and eccentric and she makes everyone around her feel more alive. It's not every day that we meet a woman who can do that.

The Life and Times of Truman Capote

Truman (Persons) Capote always felt the most at home when he was the center of attention. Born in New Orleans in 1924 to a troubled family, he was always lively and flamboyant. When he was a young boy, his mother divorced his father, Archulus Persons, and left Truman with relatives in Monroeville, Alabama, while she made a new life for herself in New York. After marrying a wealthy Cuban named Joseph Capote, she sent for Truman to live with her in New York. His new stepfather formally adopted him and changed his name to Truman Capote. Capote started writing stories when he was eight years old and, at seventeen, after graduating from high school, he began working at the *New Yorker*. He loved to shock people with his wit and his fashion, but while his personality and clothing attracted a lot of attention it was his writing that left a lasting impression. In 1948, he published his first novel, *Other Voices, Other Rooms,* and won the O'Henry Award. His most famous novel is arguably *In Cold Blood*, but his genius for poetic storytelling and creating vivid characters is never more evident than it is in *Breakfast at Tiffany's*. Capote admitted often that, of all the characters he created, Holly Golightly was his favorite. In 1984, while living in Los Angeles, Capote died of liver disease.

--- From *Breakfast at Tiffany's* ---

On the way home I noticed a cab-driver crowd gathered in front of P. J. Clark's saloon, apparently attracted there by a happy group of whiskey-eyed Australian army officers baritoning, "Waltzing Matilda." As they sang they took turns spin-dancing a girl over the cobbles under the El; and the girl, Miss Golightly, to be sure, floated round in their arms light as a scarf.

But if Miss Golightly remained unconscious of my existence, except as a doorbell convenience, I became, through the summer, rather an authority on hers. I discovered, from observing the trash-basket outside her door, that her regular reading consisted of tabloids and travel folders and astrological charts; that she smoked an esoteric cigarette called Picayunes; survived on cottage cheese and Melba toast; that her vari-colored hair was somewhat self-induced. The same source made it evident that she received V-letters by the bale. They were always torn into strips like bookmarks. I used occasionally to pluck myself a bookmark in passing. *Remember* and *miss you* and *rain* and *please write* and *damn* and *goddamn* were the words that recurred most often on these slips; those, and *lonesome* and *love*.

Also, she had a cat and she played the guitar. On days when the sun was strong, she would wash her hair, and together with the cat, a red tiger-striped tom, sit out on the fire escape thumbing a guitar while her hair dried. Whenever I heard the music, I would go stand quietly by my window. She played very well, and sometimes sang too. Sang in the hoarse, breaking tones of a boy's adolescent voice. She knew all the show hits, Cole Porter and Kurt Weill; especially she liked the songs from *Oklahoma!*, which were new that summer and everywhere. But there were moments when she played songs that made you wonder where she learned them, where indeed she came from. Harsh-tender wandering tunes with words that smacked of pineywoods or prairie. One went: *Don't wanna sleep, Don't wanna die, Just wanna go a-travelin' through the pastures of the sky*; and this one seemed to gratify her the most, for often she continued it long after her hair had dried, after the sun had gone and there were lighted windows in the dusk.

But our acquaintance did not make headway until September, an evening with the first ripple-chills of autumn running through it. I'd been to a movie, come home and gone to bed with a bourbon nightcap and the newest Simenon: so much my idea of comfort that I couldn't understand a sense of unease that multiplied until I could hear my heart beating. It was a feeling I'd read about, written about, but never before experienced. The feeling of being watched. Of someone in the room. Then: an abrupt rapping at the window, a glimpse of ghostly gray: I spilled the bourbon. It was some little while before I could bring myself to open the window, and ask Miss Golightly what she wanted.

"I've got the most terrifying man downstairs," she said, stepping off the fire escape into the room. "I mean he's sweet when he isn't drunk, but let him start lapping up the vino, and oh God quel beast! If there's one thing I loathe, it's men who bite." She loosened a gray flannel robe off her shoulder to show me evidence of what happens if a man bites. The robe was all she was wearing. "I'm sorry if I frightened you. But when the beast got so tiresome I just went out the window. I think he thinks I'm in the bathroom, not that I give a damn what he thinks, the hell with him, he'll get tired, he'll go to sleep, my God he should, eight martinis before dinner and enough wine to wash an elephant. Listen, you can throw me out if you want to. I've got a gall barging in on you like this. But that fire escape was damned icy. And you looked so cozy. Like my brother Fred. We used to sleep four in a bed, and he was the only one that ever let me hug him on a cold night. By the way, do you mind if I call you Fred?" She'd come completely into the room now, and she paused there, staring at me. I'd never seen her before not wearing dark glasses, and it was obvious now that they were prescription lenses, for without them her eyes had an assessing squint, like a jeweler's. They were large eyes, a little blue, a little green, dotted with bits of brown: vari-colored, like her hair; and, like her hair, they gave out a lively warm light. "I suppose you think I'm very brazen. Or *très fou*. Or something."

Novel Knowledge: AUDREY HEPBURN
OR MARILYN MONROE?

Capote was never happy with the choice of Audrey Hepburn as Holly Golightly for the movie based on his novel. He had his heart set on Marilyn Monroe to play the part.

"Not at all."

She seemed disappointed. "Yes, you do. Everybody does. I don't mind. It's useful."

She sat down on one of the rickety red-velvet chairs, curved her legs underneath her, and glanced round the room, her eyes puckering more pronouncedly. "How can you bear it? It's a chamber of horrors."

"Oh, you get used to anything," I said, annoyed with myself, for actually I was proud of the place.

"I don't. I'll never get used to anything. Anybody that does, they might as well be dead." Her dispraising eyes surveyed the room again. "What do you *do* here all day?"

I motioned toward a table tall with books and paper. "Write things."

"I thought writers were quite old. Of course Saroyan isn't old. I met him at a party, and really he isn't old at all. In fact," she mused, "if he'd give himself a closer shave . . . by the way, is Hemingway old?"

Novel Knowledge: WHO IS HOLLY GOLIGHTLY?

Capote said he largely based Holly Golightly on a few women he knew—Gloria Vanderbilt, Carol Grace (Walter Matthau's wife), and Oona Chaplin. Those who knew Truman Capote well, however, say Holly Golightly bears a strong likeness to the author himself.

"In his forties, I should think."

"That's not bad. I can't get excited by a man until he's forty-two. I know this idiot girl who keeps telling me I ought to go to a head-shrinker; she says I have a father complex. Which is so much *merde.* I simply *trained* myself to like older men, and it was the smartest thing I ever did. How old is W. Somerset Maugham?"

"I'm not sure. Sixty-something."

"That's not bad. I've never been to bed with a writer. No, wait: do you know Benny Shacklett?" She frowned when I shook my head. "That's funny. He's written an awful lot of radio stuff. But quel rat. Tell me, are you a real writer?"

"It depends on what you mean by real."

"Well, darling, does anyone *buy* what you write?"

"Not yet."

"I'm going to help you," she said. "I can too. Think of all the people I know who know people. I'm going to help you because you look like my brother Fred. Only smaller. I haven't seen him since I was fourteen, that's when I left home, and he was already six-feet-two. My other brothers were more your size, runts. It was the peanut butter that made Fred so tall. Everybody thought it was dotty, the way he gorged himself on peanut butter; he didn't care about anything in this world except horses and peanut butter. But he wasn't dotty, just sweet and vague and terribly slow; he'd been in the eighth grade three years when I ran away. Poor Fred. I wonder if the Army's generous with their peanut butter. Which reminds me, I'm starving."

I pointed to a bowl of apples, at the same time asked her how and why she'd left home so young. She looked at me blankly, and rubbed her nose, as though it tickled: a gesture, seeing often repeated, I came to recognize as a signal that one was trespassing. Like many people with a bold fondness for volunteering intimate information, anything that suggested a direct question, a pinning-down, put her on guard. She took a bite of apple, and said: "Tell me something you've written. The story part."

"That's one of the troubles. They're not the kind of stories you *can* tell."

"Too dirty?"

"Maybe I'll let you read one sometime."

"Whiskey and apples go together. Fix me a drink, darling. Then you can read me a story yourself."

Very few authors, especially the unpublished, can resist an invitation to read aloud. I made us both a drink and, settling in a chair opposite, began to read to her, my voice a little shaky with a combination of stage fright and enthusiasm: it was a new story, I'd finished it the day before, and that inevitable sense of shortcoming had not had time to develop. It was about two women who share a house, schoolteachers, one of whom, when the other becomes engaged, spreads with anonymous notes a scandal that prevents the marriage. As I read, each glimpse I stole of Holly made my heart contract. She fidgeted. She picked apart the butts in an ashtray, she mooned over her fingernails, as though longing for a file; worse, when I did seem to have her interest, there was actually a telltale frost over her eyes, as if she were wondering whether to buy a pair of shoes she'd seen in some window.

"Is that the *end?*" she asked, waking up. She floundered for something more to say. "Of course I like dykes themselves. They don't scare me a bit. But stories about dykes bore the bejesus out of me. I just can't put myself in their shoes. Well really, darling," she said, because I was clearly puzzled, "if it's not about a couple of old bulldykes, what the hell *is* it about?"

But I was in no mood to compound the mistake of having read the story with the further embarrassment of explaining it. The same vanity that had led to such exposure, now forced me to mark her down as an insensitive mindless show-off.

"Incidentally," she said, "do you happen to *know* any nice lesbians? I'm looking for a roommate. Well, don't laugh. I'm so disorganized, I simply can't afford a maid; and really, dykes are wonderful home-makers, they love to do all the work, you never have to bother about brooms and defrosting and sending out the laundry. I had a roommate in Hollywood, she played in Westerns, they called her the Lone Ranger; but I'll say this for her, she was better than a man around the house. Of course people couldn't help but think I must be a bit of a dyke myself. And of course I am. Everyone is: a bit. So what? That never discouraged a man yet, in fact, it seems to goad them on . . . "

Ántonia Shimerda

IN *MY ÁNTONIA* BY WILLA CATHER
FIRST PUBLISHED IN: 1918

Who is she? A hard-working farm girl determined to call America home.

Her Story

Ántonia Shimerda is the toughest, most tenacious farm girl in the Great Plains. She has to be, or else she might not survive. Ántonia has not lived in the United States for long; her family only recently packed up their lives and left their Bohemian homeland (what is today the Czech Republic) to start over in Nebraska. But, when Jimmy Burden comes to live with his grandparents, the two become, for a lack of other kids their own age, instant friends.

Ántonia's story is told through Jimmy's eyes. He sees his sweet childhood friend grow into a pioneering woman. Time and again, he is amazed by her fortitude. She endures long, cold winters with little heat and works the fields under the hot July sun with little relief. When the farm and family suffer setback after setback, Ántonia's father feels the weight of failure and puts a gun to his head. With Mr. Shimerda dead, Ántonia forges ahead, even more determined to make the harsh land a place that she and her family can call home.

What Makes Ántonia Shimerda So Memorable?

Jimmy Burden says, "Ántonia had always been one to leave images in the mind that did not fade—that grew stronger with time." He's right. Her spirit represents—and forces Americans to remember—all of the strong-willed immigrants at the turn of the twentieth century who settled the harsh Great Plains before there were even fences; she is a magnificent and stark reminder of their courage and tenacity. The harshness of her life does not diminish her spirit. Ántonia's resilience is incredible and enviable. For if she can endure so much and find so much happiness in her life, it seems that the rest of us should, at the very least, be able to try.

The Life and Times of Willa Cather

Willa Cather, born in Virginia in 1873, moved with her family to Nebraska when she was nine years old. Her family was not wealthy, but she insisted on going to college so they borrowed money and sent her to the University of Nebraska. Fascinated by botany and astronomy, Willa planned to study science at the university, but after she won an essay contest she turned her attention to writing instead.

When offered a job with *McClure Magazine*, the small-town girl packed up and moved to New York, which is where she lived for the rest of her life. While at *McClure* she wrote her first novel, *Alexander's Bridge*. In 1908, she took over as managing editor for *McClure*, but she continued writing novels and won the Pulitzer Prize in 1923 for *One of Ours*.

Novel Knowledge: A Private Woman

In an effort to maintain as much privacy as possible Willa Cather destroyed her manuscript drafts and personal letters. In her will, she restricted scholars from using quotes from any of her personal papers that were not destroyed.

Cather was a fiercely private person, so little is known about her personal life. It seems that she mostly had relationships with women, but whether they were romantic is unknown. She lived with her friend Edith Lewis for thirty-five years and died in 1947 at the age of seventy.

From *My Ántonia*

As we approached the Shimerdas' dwelling, I could still see nothing but rough red hillocks, and draws with shelving banks and long roots hanging out where the earth had crumbled away. Presently, against one of those banks, I saw a sort of shed, thatched with the same wine-coloured grass that grew everywhere. Near it tilted a shattered windmill frame, that had no wheel. We drove up to this skeleton to tie our horses, and then I saw a door and window sunk deep in the drawbank. The door stood open, and a woman and a girl of fourteen ran out and looked up at us hopefully. A little girl trailed along behind them. The woman had on her head the same embroidered shawl with silk fringes that she wore when she had alighted from the train at Black Hawk. She was not old, but she was certainly not young. Her face was alert and lively, with a sharp chin and shrewd little eyes. She shook grandmother's hand energetically.

'Very glad, very glad!' she ejaculated. Immediately she pointed to the bank out of which she had emerged and said, 'House no good, house no good!'

Grandmother nodded consolingly. 'You'll get fixed up comfortable after while, Mrs. Shimerda; make good house.'

My grandmother always spoke in a very loud tone to foreigners, as if they were deaf. She made Mrs. Shimerda understand the friendly intention of our visit, and the Bohemian woman handled the loaves of bread and even smelled them, and examined the pies with lively curiosity, exclaiming, 'Much good, much thank!'—and again she wrung grandmother's hand.

The oldest son, Ambroz—they called it Ambrosch—came out of the cave and stood beside his mother. He was nineteen years old, short and broad-backed, with a close-cropped, flat head, and a wide, flat face. His hazel eyes were little and shrewd, like his mother's, but more sly and suspicious; they fairly snapped at the food. The family had been living on corncakes and sorghum molasses for three days.

Novel Knowledge: MODEST SALES

When the story of Ántonia was published, critics loved it, but sales were modest. Though *My Ántonia* is not the work that won Willa Cather the Pulitzer Prize, it is considered one of the greatest novels in American literature.

The little girl was pretty, but Ántonia—they accented the name thus, strongly, when they spoke to her—was still prettier. I remembered what the conductor had said about her eyes. They were big and warm and full of light, like the sun shining on brown pools in the wood. Her skin was brown, too, and in her cheeks she had a glow of rich, dark colour. Her brown hair was curly and wild-looking.
* * *

When the sun was dropping low, Ántonia came up the big south draw with her team. How much older she had grown in eight months! She had come to us a child, and now she was a tall, strong young girl, although her fifteenth birthday had just slipped by. I ran out and met her as she brought her horses up to the windmill to water them. She wore the boots her father had so thoughtfully taken off before he shot himself, and his old fur cap. Her out-grown cotton dress switched about her calves, over the boot-tops. She kept her sleeves rolled up all day, and her arms and throat were burned as brown as a sailor's. Her neck came up strongly out of her shoulders, like the bole of a tree out of the turf. One sees that draught-horse neck among the peasant women in all old countries.

She greeted me gaily, and began at once to tell me how much ploughing she had done that day. Ambrosch, she said, was on the north quarter, breaking sod with the oxen.

'Jim, you ask Jake how much he ploughed to-day. I don't want that Jake get more done in one day than me. I want we have very much corn this fall.'

While the horses drew in the water, and nosed each other, and then drank again, Ántonia sat down on the windmill step and rested her head on her hand.

'You see the big prairie fire from your place last night? I hope your grandpa ain't lose no stacks?'

'No, we didn't. I came to ask you something, Tony. Grandmother wants to know if you can't go to the term of school that begins next week over at the sod schoolhouse. She says there's a good teacher, and you'd learn a lot.'

Ántonia stood up, lifting and dropping her shoulders as if they were stiff. 'I ain't got time to learn. I can work like mans now. My mother can't say no more how Ambrosch do all and nobody to help him. I can work as much as him. School is all right for little boys. I help make this land one good farm.'

She clucked to her team and started for the barn. I walked beside her, feeling vexed. Was she going to grow up boastful like her mother, I wondered? Before we reached the stable, I felt something tense in her silence, and glancing up I saw that she was crying. She turned her face from me and looked off at the red streak of dying light, over the dark prairie.

I climbed up into the loft and threw down the hay for her, while she unharnessed her team. We walked slowly back toward the house. Ambrosch had come in from the north quarter, and was watering his oxen at the tank.

Ántonia took my hand. 'Sometime you will tell me all those nice things you learn at the school, won't you, Jimmy?' she asked with a sudden rush of feeling in her voice.

* * *

After supper I rode home through the sad, soft spring twilight. Since winter I had seen very little of Ántonia. She was out in the fields from sunup until sundown. If I rode over to see her where she was ploughing, she stopped at the end of a row to chat for a moment, then gripped her plough-handles, clucked to her team, and waded on down the furrow, making me feel that she was now grown up and had no time for me. On Sundays she helped her mother make garden or sewed all day. Grandfather was pleased with Ántonia. When we complained of her, he only smiled and said, 'She will help some fellow get ahead in the world.'

Nowadays Tony could talk of nothing but the prices of things, or how much she could lift and endure. She was too proud of her strength. I knew, too, that Ambrosch put upon her some chores a girl ought not to do, and that the farm-hands around the country joked in a nasty way about it. Whenever I saw her come up the furrow, shouting to her beasts, sunburned, sweaty, her dress open at the neck, and her throat and chest dust-plastered, I used to think of the tone in which poor Mr. Shimerda, who could say so little, yet managed to say so much when he exclaimed, 'My Ántonia!'

* * *

I told Ántonia I would come back, but life intervened, and it was twenty years before I kept my promise…

'I can't believe it's you, sitting here, in my own kitchen. You wouldn't have known me, would you, Jim? You've kept so young, yourself. But it's easier for a man. I can't see how my Anton looks any older than the day I married him. His teeth have kept so nice. I haven't got many left. But I feel just as young as I used to, and I can do as much work. Oh, we don't have to work so hard now! We've got plenty to help us, papa and me. And how many have you got, Jim?'

When I told her I had no children, she seemed embarrassed. 'Oh, ain't that too bad! Maybe you could take one of my bad ones, now? That Leo; he's the worst of all.' She leaned toward me with a smile. 'And I love him the best,' she whispered.

'Mother!' the two girls murmured reproachfully from the dishes.

Ántonia threw up her head and laughed. 'I can't help it. You know I do. Maybe it's because he came on Easter Day, I don't know. And he's never out of mischief one minute!'

I was thinking, as I watched her, how little it mattered—about her teeth, for instance. I know so many women who have kept all the things that she had lost, but whose inner glow has faded. Whatever else was gone, Ántonia had not lost the fire of life. Her skin, so brown and hardened, had not that look of flabbiness, as if the sap beneath it had been secretly drawn away.

While we were talking, the little boy whom they called Jan came in and sat down on the step beside Nina, under the hood of the stairway. He wore a funny long gingham apron, like a smock, over his trousers, and his hair was clipped so short that his head looked white and naked. He watched us out of his big, sorrowful grey eyes.

'He wants to tell you about the dog, mother. They found it dead,' Anna said, as she passed us on her way to the cupboard.

Ántonia beckoned the boy to her. He stood by her chair, leaning his elbows on her knees and twisting her apron strings in his slender fingers, while he told her his story softly in Bohemian, and the tears brimmed over and hung on his long lashes. His mother listened, spoke soothingly to him and in a whisper promised him something that made him give her a quick, teary smile. He slipped away and whispered his secret to Nina, sitting close to her and talking behind his hand.

When Anna finished her work and had washed her hands, she came and stood behind her mother's chair. 'Why don't we show Mr. Burden our new fruit cave?' she asked.

We started off across the yard with the children at our heels. The boys were standing by the windmill, talking about the dog; some of them ran ahead to open the cellar door. When we descended, they all came down after us, and seemed quite as proud of the cave as the girls were.

* * *

I lay awake for a long while, until the slow-moving moon passed my window on its way up the heavens. I was thinking about Ántonia and her children; about Anna's solicitude for her, Ambrosch's grave affection, Leo's jealous, animal little love. That moment, when they all came tumbling out of the cave into the light, was a sight any man might have come far to see. Ántonia had always been one to leave images in the mind that did not fade—that grew stronger with time. In my memory there was a succession of such pictures, fixed there like the old woodcuts of one's first primer: Ántonia kicking her bare legs against the sides of my pony when we came home in triumph with our snake; Ántonia in her black shawl and fur cap, as she stood by her father's grave in the snowstorm; Ántonia coming in with her work-team along the evening sky-line. She lent herself to immemorial human attitudes which we recognize by instinct as universal and true. I had not been mistaken. She was a battered woman now, not a lovely girl; but she still had that something which fires the imagination, could still stop one's breath for a moment by a look or gesture that somehow revealed the meaning in common things. She had only to stand in the orchard, to put her hand on a little crab tree and look up at the apples, to make you feel the goodness of planting and tending and harvesting at last. All the strong things of her heart came out in her body, that had been so tireless in serving generous emotions.

It was no wonder that her sons stood tall and straight. She was a rich mine of life, like the founders of early races.

Edna Pontellier

IN *THE AWAKENING* BY KATE CHOPIN
FIRST PUBLISHED IN: 1899

Who is she? A daring woman who decides to live the life she wants rather than the life society expects of her.

Her Story

Edna Pontellier is a free-spirited woman living an empty life. At twenty-eight, she's done what is expected of her. She's married a respectable, successful businessman and has given birth to two children. But despite meeting societal expectations, she has always felt that something was missing in her life. These feelings intensify when she and her family go to Grand Isles for the summer and she meets a young man named Robert LeBrun. Edna does little to hide her feelings toward Robert, and does even less to hide her lack of feelings for her husband. It's an affair waiting to happen as Robert awakens a sexual desire in Edna that she has never felt for her husband. More important, Edna begins to imagine a life that is defined by her own desires, rather than by her husband and children. Drawn to the prospect of a more passionate life, she chooses to follow her desires without question.

Novel Knowledge: THE LOYAL HUSBAND

Oscar Chopin was a man ahead of his time. He encouraged Kate to write and think for herself. By all accounts and evidence, it seems he admired her spunk and treated her as an equal, which was practically unheard of at the time.

What Makes Edna Pontellier So Memorable?

Edna speaks her mind and follows her heart. She doesn't care what people think. When asked if she would be going abroad with her husband, something that would have been assumed of other women, Edna says, "I'm not going to be forced into doing things. I don't want to go abroad. I want to be let alone."

Perhaps most shocking is her attitude toward her children. She is not neglectful, but Edna fears that motherhood will strip her of any other identity. The kids will grow, leave her, and she will have nothing if she doesn't have her own self. Even today, her decision to move out of her house and live separately from her children is considered a bold and disturbing display of independence.

Whatever we might think of Edna Pontellier, free-spirited or selfish, one thing is certain—she tried to live the life she wanted. She tried to be happy. For that, it's hard to forget her.

The Life and Times of Kate Chopin

Kate (O'Flaherty) Chopin, born in 1850 in St. Louis, Missouri, was a popular writer for most of her career. She lived in New Orleans with her husband, Oscar, raising their children and writing when she had the time. When Oscar died of swamp fever in 1882, he left Kate heartbroken and deep in debt. Two years later, she and her children moved back to St. Louis so she could focus on a writing career with the financial help of her wealthy mother.

Her first novel, *At Fault*, was published in 1890. Two collections of short stories followed—*Bayou Folk* and *A Night in Acadia*. Short stories such as *Désirée's Baby* and *The Story of an Hour* made her a household name. Prior to the publication of *The Awakening*, Chopin was loved by readers and respected by critics. However, readers and critics alike were turned off by Edna Pontellier's feminist leanings and dismissal of societal expectations and harshly critiqued the novel. Devastated by the criticism, Chopin felt deeply misunderstood. She did not write another book and her reputation never recovered.

From *The Awakening*

Edna Pontellier could not have told why, wishing to go to the beach with Robert, she should in the first place have declined, and in the second place have followed in obedience to one of the two contradictory impulses which impelled her.

A certain light was beginning to dawn dimly within her,—the light which, showing the way, forbids it.

At that early period it served but to bewilder her. It moved her to dreams, to thoughtfulness, to the shadowy anguish which had overcome her in the midnight when she had abandoned herself to tears.

In short, Mrs. Pontellier was beginning to realize her position in the universe as a human being, and to recognize her relations as an individual to the world within and about her. This may seem like a ponderous weight of wisdom to descend upon the soul of a young woman of twenty-eight—perhaps more wisdom than the Holy Ghost is usually pleased to vouchsafe to any woman.

But the beginning of things, of a world especially, is necessarily vague, tangled, chaotic, and exceedingly disturbing. How few of us ever emerge from such beginning! How many souls perish in its tumult!

The voice of the sea is seductive; never ceasing, whispering, clamoring, murmuring, inviting the soul to wander for a spell in abysses of solitude; to lose itself in mazes of inward contemplation.

The voice of the sea speaks to the soul. The touch of the sea is sensuous, enfolding the body in its soft, close embrace.

* * *

Novel Knowledge: BACKLASH FROM *THE AWAKENING*

By creating Edna Pontellier, Chopin ruined her career. Prior to *The Awakening* she had enjoyed fame, success, and praise from readers and critics. Once *The Awakening* was published, however, she had to deal with the public's shock and outrage. Her hometown paper, the *St. Louis Post-Dispatched,* described the novel as "poison." Deeply hurt and misunderstood, Chopin never wrote again, and *The Awakening* was all but forgotten until the 1960s.

Mrs. Pontellier was not a woman given to confidences, a characteristic hitherto contrary to her nature. Even as a child she had lived her own small life all within herself. At a very early period she had apprehended instinctively the dual life—that outward existence which conforms, the inward life which questions.

That summer at Grand Isle she began to loosen a little the mantle of reserve that had always enveloped her. There may have been—there must have been—influences, both subtle and apparent, working in their several ways to induce her to do this; but the most obvious was the influence of Adele Ratignolle. The excessive physical charm of the Creole had first attracted her, for Edna had a sensuous susceptibility to beauty. Then the candor of the woman's whole existence, which every one might read, and which formed so striking a contrast to her own habitual reserve—this might have furnished a link. Who can tell what metals the gods use in forging the subtle bond which we call sympathy, which we might as well call love.

The two women went away one morning to the beach together, arm in arm, under the huge white sunshade. Edna had prevailed upon Madame Ratignolle to leave the children behind, though she could not induce her to relinquish a diminutive roll of needlework, which Adele begged to be allowed to slip into the depths of her pocket. In some unaccountable way they had escaped from Robert.

* * *

Her marriage to Leonce Pontellier was purely an accident, in this respect resembling many other marriages which masquerade as the decrees of Fate. It was in the midst of her secret great passion that she met him. He fell in love, as men are in the habit of doing, and pressed his suit with an earnestness and an ardor which left nothing to be desired. He pleased her; his absolute devotion flattered her. She fancied there was a sympathy of thought and taste between them, in which fancy she was mistaken. Add to this the violent opposition of her father and her sister Margaret to her marriage with a Catholic, and we need seek no further for the motives which led her to accept Monsieur Pontellier for her husband.

The acme of bliss, which would have been a marriage with the tragedian, was not for her in this world. As the devoted wife of a man who worshiped her, she felt she would take her place with a certain dignity in the world of reality, closing the portals forever behind her upon the realm of romance and dreams.

But it was not long before the tragedian had gone to join the cavalry officer and the engaged young man and a few others; and Edna found herself face to face with the realities. She grew fond of her husband, realizing with some unaccountable satisfaction that no trace of passion or excessive and fictitious warmth colored her affection, thereby threatening its dissolution.

She was fond of her children in an uneven, impulsive way. She would sometimes gather them passionately to her heart; she would sometimes forget them. The year before they had spent part of the summer with their grandmother Pontellier in Iberville. Feeling secure regarding their happiness and welfare, she did not miss them except with an occasional intense longing. Their absence was a sort of relief, though she did not admit this, even to herself. It seemed to free her of a responsibility which she had blindly assumed and for which Fate had not fitted her.

Edna did not reveal so much as all this to Madame Ratignolle that summer day when they sat with faces turned to the sea. But a good part of it escaped her. She had put her head down on Madame Ratignolle's shoulder. She was flushed and felt intoxicated with the sound of her own voice and the unaccustomed taste of candor. It muddled her like wine, or like a first breath of freedom.

* * *

Edna still felt dazed when she got outside in the open air. The Doctor's coupe had returned for him and stood before the porte cochere. She did not wish to enter the coupe, and told Doctor Mandelet she would walk; she was not afraid, and would go alone. He directed his carriage to meet him at Mrs. Pontellier's, and he started to walk home with her.

Up—away up, over the narrow street between the tall houses, the stars were blazing. The air was mild and caressing, but cool with the breath of spring and the night. They walked slowly, the Doctor with a heavy, measured tread and his hands behind him; Edna, in an absent-minded way, as she had walked one night at Grand Isle, as if her thoughts had gone ahead of her and she was striving to overtake them.

"You shouldn't have been there, Mrs. Pontellier," he said. "That was no place for you. Adele is full of whims at such times. There were a dozen women she might have had with her, unimpressionable women. I felt that it was cruel, cruel. You shouldn't have gone."

"Oh, well!" she answered, indifferently. "I don't know that it matters after all. One has to think of the children some time or other; the sooner the better."

"When is Leonce coming back?"

"Quite soon. Some time in March."

"And you are going abroad?"

"Perhaps—no, I am not going. I'm not going to be forced into doing things. I don't want to go abroad. I want to be let alone. Nobody has any right—except children, perhaps—and even then, it seems to me—or it did seem—" She felt that her speech was voicing the incoherency of her thoughts, and stopped abruptly.

"The trouble is," sighed the Doctor, grasping her meaning intuitively, "that youth is given up to illusions. It seems to be a provision of Nature; a decoy to secure mothers for the race. And Nature takes no account of moral consequences, of arbitrary conditions which we create, and which we feel obliged to maintain at any cost."

"Yes," she said. "The years that are gone seem like dreams—if one might go on sleeping and dreaming—but to wake up and find— oh! well! perhaps it is better to wake up after all, even to suffer, rather than to remain a dupe to illusions all one's life."

"It seems to me, my dear child," said the Doctor at parting, holding her hand, "you seem to me to be in trouble. I am not going to ask for your confidence. I will only say that if ever you feel moved to give it to me, perhaps I might help you. I know I would understand, And I tell you there are not many who would—not many, my dear."

"Some way I don't feel moved to speak of things that trouble me. Don't think I am ungrateful or that I don't appreciate your sympathy. There are periods of despondency and suffering which take possession of me. But I don't want anything but my own way. That is wanting a good deal, of course, when you have to trample upon the lives, the hearts, the prejudices of others—but no matter-still, I shouldn't want to trample upon the little lives. Oh! I don't know what I'm saying, Doctor. Good night. Don't blame me for anything."

"Yes, I will blame you if you don't come and see me soon. We will talk of things you never have dreamt of talking about before. It will do us both good. I don't want you to blame yourself, whatever comes. Good night, my child."

She let herself in at the gate, but instead of entering she sat upon the step of the porch. The night was quiet and soothing. All the tearing emotion of the last few hours seemed to fall away from her like a somber, uncomfortable garment, which she had but to loosen to be rid of. She went back to that hour before Adele had sent for her; and her senses kindled afresh in thinking of Robert's words, the pressure of his arms, and the feeling of his lips upon her own. She could picture at that moment no greater bliss on earth than possession of the beloved one. His expression of love had already given him to her in part. When she thought that he was there at hand, waiting for her, she grew numb with the intoxication of expectancy. It was so late; he would be asleep perhaps. She would awaken him with a kiss. She hoped he would be asleep that she might arouse him with her caresses.

Still, she remembered Adele's voice whispering, "Think of the children; think of them." She meant to think of them; that determination had driven into her soul like a death wound—but not to-night. To-morrow would be time to think of everything.

Robert was not waiting for her in the little parlor. He was nowhere at hand. The house was empty. But he had scrawled on a piece of paper that lay in the lamplight:

"I love you. Good-by—because I love you."

Edna grew faint when she read the words. She went and sat on the sofa. Then she stretched herself out there, never uttering a sound. She did not sleep. She did not go to bed. The lamp sputtered and went out. She was still awake in the morning, when Celestine unlocked the kitchen door and came in to light the fire.

Amy Dorrit

IN *LITTLE DORRIT* BY CHARLES DICKENS
FIRST PUBLISHED IN: 1855–1857

Who is she? A pragmatic, compassionate woman not easily swayed by wealth or social standing.

Her Story

Amy Dorrit was born and raised in prison. Her father's financial problems forced the entire Dorrit family into the Marshelsea, a debtor's prison, while Amy was still in her mother's womb. A slight girl with a soft voice and a tender smile, Amy is known to everyone as "Little Dorrit." As she grows up, she comes and goes from the prison as she pleases, but always returns to her father's cell before the prison gates are locked for the night. With her mother dead, she devotes her life to caring for her father.

By day, Amy works for an agitated, old woman named Mrs. Clennam. Mrs. Clennam's son, Arthur, is struck by how kind his mother is to the young woman. She has never been kind to anyone—not even him or his father. In his search for some explanation of his mother's kindness, he learns about Amy's life in the prison. His search also reveals an inheritance the Dorrit family should have received years ago. After twenty years in the debtor's prison, Amy's father is free and wealthy.

With her newfound wealth, Amy should be happy. But the money only makes her miserable. When the Dorrit family goes to Italy (because all wealthy English families go to Italy), Amy doesn't know what to do with herself. She misses her friends back at the Marshelsea and she misses her life as it was. Most of all, she misses Arthur, whom she has come to love. It never occurs to Arthur, however, that Little Dorrit, a woman half his age, could have feelings for him. When a banking scam causes the Dorrits—and Arthur—to lose their wealth, Amy is relieved to be rid of the money, but Arthur does not take to poverty as well. When Amy visits Arthur in the debtor's prison, she feels as though she is back where she belongs—in prison, caring for a man she loves.

What Makes Amy Dorrit So Memorable?

Amy Dorrit is industrious, pragmatic, and insightful. Yet, her most memorable qualities are her modesty and deep compassion for others. Her ability to rise above all the pettiness that lies around her is inspiring. By remaining who she is and keeping her senses in spite of the silliness wealth tends to breed, Amy is the most admirable of all the Dorrits and among the most unforgettable of Dickens's characters. She is, after all, the only heroine for whom Dickens titled a novel!

The Life and Times of Charles Dickens

Charles Dickens was a natural-born storyteller with gifts for creating unforgettable characters. Born in 1812 in Portsmouth, Hampshire, England, Charles's life began as one of privilege. His father, John Dickens, was a good man, but one unable to live within his means. When John was sent to debtor's prison, Charles supported the family by working at a shoe blacking factory. He was twelve. By the time he was a teenager, he had lived in two vastly different worlds—that of the well-to-do and that of the working poor.

In 1836, he became editor for *Bentley's Miscellany* and married Catherine Hogarth. He and Catherine lived in London and had ten children together. Americans loved him and so he ventured to the States in 1842 for a lengthy book tour. He loved traveling and meeting people so he did not mind touring. His energy, it seemed, was boundless. That all changed however in 1865 when Dickens was in a train crash now known as the Staplehurst Railway Accident. While returning to London from France, the train derailed and much of the train went over a cliff. While Dickens was hailed as a hero for rescuing dying and injured passengers, the wreck set his nerves on edge and deeply troubled him for the rest of his life. Some believe the psychological effects of the accident aged him considerably and contributed to his death five years later. He is buried in Poet's Corner of Westminster Abbey, London.

From *Little Dorrit*

The night was dark; and the prison lamps in the yard, and the candles in the prison windows faintly shining behind many sorts of wry old curtain and blind, had not the air of making it lighter. A few people loitered about, but the greater part of the population was within doors. The old man, taking the right-hand side of the yard, turned in at the third or fourth doorway, and began to ascend the stairs. 'They are rather dark, sir, but you will not find anything in the way.'

He paused for a moment before opening a door on the second story. He had no sooner turned the handle than the visitor saw Little Dorrit, and saw the reason of her setting so much store by dining alone.

She had brought the meat home that she should have eaten herself, and was already warming it on a gridiron over the fire for her father, clad in an old grey gown and a black cap, awaiting his supper at the table. A clean cloth was spread before him, with knife, fork, and spoon, salt-cellar, pepper-box, glass, and pewter ale-pot.

Such zests as his particular little phial of cayenne pepper and his pennyworth of pickles in a saucer, were not wanting.

Novel Knowledge: THE PUBLIC LOVED HER

The public became wrapped up in Little Dorrit's life from the first installment and waited anxiously each month for the next chapter. Few writers, during this time, did so much to humanize women and give them a voice as Charles Dickens did.

She started, coloured deeply, and turned white. The visitor, more with his eyes than by the slight impulsive motion of his hand, entreated her to be reassured and to trust him.

'I found this gentleman,' said the uncle—'Mr Clennam, William, son of Amy's friend—at the outer gate, wishful, as he was going by, of paying his respects, but hesitating whether to come in or not. This is my brother William, sir.'

'I hope,' said Arthur, very doubtful what to say, 'that my respect for your daughter may explain and justify my desire to be presented to you, sir.'

'Mr Clennam,' returned the other, rising, taking his cap off in the flat of his hand, and so holding it, ready to put on again, 'you do me honour. You are welcome, sir;' with a low bow. 'Frederick, a chair. Pray sit down, Mr Clennam.'

He put his black cap on again as he had taken it off, and resumed his own seat. There was a wonderful air of benignity and patronage in his manner. These were the ceremonies with which he received the collegians.

'You are welcome to the Marshalsea, sir. I have welcomed many gentlemen to these walls. Perhaps you are aware—my daughter Amy may have mentioned that I am the Father of this place.'

'I—so I have understood,' said Arthur, dashing at the assertion.

'You know, I dare say, that my daughter Amy was born here. A good girl, sir, a dear girl, and long a comfort and support to me. Amy, my dear, put this dish on; Mr Clennam will excuse the primitive customs to which we are reduced here. Is it a compliment to ask you if you would do me the honour, sir, to—'

Novel Knowledge: The Inspiration for Amy Dorrit

In 1846, a wealthy heir to a banking fortune asked Dickens to set up a home for women who needed help getting back on their feet. Dickens accepted the request and called it The Urania Cottage. The Cottage had strict rules but gave women a safe place to learn and slowly return to society. Dickens was deeply involved in interviewing the women and deciding who would stay at the home. Many scholars believe Amy Dorrit was based on the women Dickens interviewed.

'Thank you,' returned Arthur. 'Not a morsel.'

He felt himself quite lost in wonder at the manner of the man, and that the probability of his daughter's having had a reserve as to her family history, should be so far out of his mind.

She filled his glass, put all the little matters on the table ready to his hand, and then sat beside him while he ate his supper. Evidently in observance of their nightly custom, she put some bread before herself, and touched his glass with her lips; but Arthur saw she was troubled and took nothing. Her look at her father, half admiring him and proud of him, half ashamed for him, all devoted and loving, went to his inmost heart.

The Father of the Marshalsea condescended towards his brother as an amiable, well-meaning man; a private character, who had not arrived at distinction. 'Frederick,' said he, 'you and Fanny sup at your lodgings to-night, I know. What have you done with Fanny, Frederick?' 'She is walking with Tip.'

'Tip—as you may know—is my son, Mr Clennam. He has been a little wild, and difficult to settle, but his introduction to the world was rather'—he shrugged his shoulders with a faint sigh, and looked round the room—'a little adverse. Your first visit here, sir?'

'My first.'

'You could hardly have been here since your boyhood without my knowledge. It very seldom happens that anybody—of any pretensions—any pretensions—comes here without being presented to me.'

'As many as forty or fifty in a day have been introduced to my brother,' said Frederick, faintly lighting up with a ray of pride.

'Yes!' the Father of the Marshalsea assented. 'We have even exceeded that number. On a fine Sunday in term time, it is quite a Levee—quite a Levee. Amy, my dear, I have been trying half the day to remember the name of the gentleman from Camberwell who was introduced to me last Christmas week by that agreeable coal-merchant who was remanded for six months.'

'I don't remember his name, father.'

'Frederick, do you remember his name?' Frederick doubted if he had ever heard it. No one could doubt that Frederick was the last person upon earth to put such a question to, with any hope of information.

'I mean,' said his brother, 'the gentleman who did that handsome action with so much delicacy. Ha! Tush! The name has quite escaped me. Mr Clennam, as I have happened to mention handsome and delicate action, you may like, perhaps, to know what it was.'

'Very much,' said Arthur, withdrawing his eyes from the delicate head beginning to droop and the pale face with a new solicitude stealing over it.

'It is so generous, and shows so much fine feeling, that it is almost a duty to mention it. I said at the time that I always would mention it on every suitable occasion, without regard to personal sensitiveness. A—well—a—it's of no use to disguise the fact—you must know, Mr Clennam, that it does sometimes occur that people who come here desire to offer some little—Testimonial—to the Father of the place.'

To see her hand upon his arm in mute entreaty half-repressed, and her timid little shrinking figure turning away, was to see a sad, sad sight.

* * *

She had slipped out after the rest, and they were alone. 'Not on any account,' said the visitor, hurriedly. 'Pray allow me to—' chink, chink, chink.

'Mr Clennam,' said the Father, 'I am deeply, deeply—' But his visitor had shut up his hand to stop the clinking, and had gone down-stairs with great speed.

He saw no Little Dorrit on his way down, or in the yard. The last
two or three stragglers were hurrying to the lodge, and he was
following, when he caught sight of her in the doorway of the first
house from the entrance. He turned back hastily.

'Pray forgive me,' he said, 'for speaking to you here; pray forgive
me for coming here at all! I followed you to-night. I did so, that I
might endeavour to render you and your family some service. You
know the terms on which I and my mother are, and may not be
surprised that I have preserved our distant relations at her house,
lest I should unintentionally make her jealous, or resentful, or do
you any injury in her estimation. What I have seen here, in this
short time, has greatly increased my heartfelt wish to be a friend to
you. It would recompense me for much disappointment if I could
hope to gain your confidence.'

She was scared at first, but seemed to take courage while he spoke
to her.

'You are very good, sir. You speak very earnestly to me. But I—but
I wish you had not watched me.'

He understood the emotion with which she said it, to arise in her
father's behalf; and he respected it, and was silent.

'Mrs Clennam has been of great service to me; I don't know what
we should have done without the employment she has given me; I
am afraid it may not be a good return to become secret with her;
I can say no more to-night, sir. I am sure you mean to be kind to
us. Thank you, thank you.'

'Let me ask you one question before I leave. Have you known my
mother long?'

'I think two years, sir,—The bell has stopped.'

'How did you know her first? Did she send here for you?'

'No. She does not even know that I live here. We have a friend, father and I—a poor labouring man, but the best of friends—and I wrote out that I wished to do needlework, and gave his address. And he got what I wrote out displayed at a few places where it cost nothing, and Mrs Clennam found me that way, and sent for me. The gate will be locked, sir!'

She was so tremulous and agitated, and he was so moved by compassion for her, and by deep interest in her story as it dawned upon him, that he could scarcely tear himself away. But the stoppage of the bell, and the quiet in the prison, were a warning to depart; and with a few hurried words of kindness he left her gliding back to her father.

But he remained too late. The inner gate was locked, and the lodge closed. After a little fruitless knocking with his hand, he was standing there with the disagreeable conviction upon him that he had got to get through the night, when a voice accosted him from behind.

'Caught, eh?' said the voice. 'You won't go home till morning. Oh! It's you, is it, Mr Clennam?'

The voice was Tip's; and they stood looking at one another in the prison-yard, as it began to rain.

'You've done it,' observed Tip; 'you must be sharper than that next time.'

'But you are locked in too,' said Arthur.

'I believe I am!' said Tip, sarcastically. 'About! But not in your way. I belong to the shop, only my sister has a theory that our governor must never know it. I don't see why, myself.'

'Can I get any shelter?' asked Arthur. 'What had I better do?'

'We had better get hold of Amy first of all,' said Tip, referring any difficulty to her as a matter of course.

'I would rather walk about all night—it's not much to do—than give that trouble.'

'You needn't do that, if you don't mind paying for a bed. If you don't mind paying, they'll make you up one on the Snuggery table, under the circumstances. If you'll come along, I'll introduce you there.'

As they passed down the yard, Arthur looked up at the window of the room he had lately left, where the light was still burning. 'Yes, sir,' said Tip, following his glance. 'That's the governor's. She'll sit with him for another hour reading yesterday's paper to him, or something of that sort; and then she'll come out like a little ghost, and vanish away without a sound.'

'I don't understand you.'

'The governor sleeps up in the room, and she has a lodging at the turnkey's. First house there,' said Tip, pointing out the doorway into which she had retired. 'First house, sky parlour. She pays twice as much for it as she would for one twice as good outside. But she stands by the governor, poor dear girl, day and night.'

Dorothea Brooke

IN *MIDDLEMARCH* BY GEORGE ELIOT
FIRST PUBLISHED IN: 1872

Who is she? An intellectual woman in search of a greater purpose in life.

Her Story

Dorothea Brooke has too much money—at least that's how she sees it—and she wants to use it to improve the lives of the poor. With her gift for architectural drawing, Dorothea comes up with a lot of good ideas for how she might do it. But no one expects anything from Dorothea other than marrying well, bearing children, and enjoying the horses she rides so beautifully.

However, when she meets Casaubon, a somber-looking man twenty-seven years older than she, Dorothea begins to see hope and meaning for her life. Casaubon leads her to believe he wants her help on an important project and she is flattered. Dorothea's family is shocked when she tells them she plans to marry Casaubon; still, they do not disapprove since his wealth and social standing is even greater than their own.

But after a brief honeymoon in Rome, Casaubon turns cold. He acts as though he never planned for Dorothea to help with his work. Frustrated and insulted, Dorothea returns to her architectural ideas and searches for opportunities to use her mind and her money (which, by law, is now Casaubon's money) for the good of her town, Middlemarch.

Matters become even more complicated when Casaubon's younger cousin Ladislaw returns to Middlemarch. Casaubon, his health failing, sees the attraction between Dorothea and Ladislaw and decides to curtail the relationship. He knows that his wife is deeply attached to her philanthropic endeavors, and alters his will in an effort to see to it that, as his widow, Dorothea will give all of her attention to her Middlemarch and none to Ladislaw.

What Makes Dorothea Brooke So Memorable?

Dorothea Brooke's philanthropic nature is inspiring. Today, a woman like Dorothea might study architecture or start a business, but in nineteenth-century England, education and enterprise are not options. Despite the limitations, Dorothea manages to find purpose in her life while improving the lives of the poor in Middlemarch.

The Life and Times of George Eliot (Mary Ann Evans)

Mary Ann Evans wanted to be a writer, but only if her writing was taken seriously. Because women were popular for writing romance—and nothing more—she felt she had to publish under a man's name; she chose the alias "George Eliot." She had political and psychological themes she wanted to weave into her stories.

Mary Ann was also reluctant to reveal her identity for fear that readers would disapprove of her personal life and stop reading her work. Her own love life was a source of continuous gossip. After a number of heartbreaking infatuations, she found love, scandalous as it was, with a married man named George Henry Lewes. Lewes never divorced his wife, but George and Mary Ann often referred to each other as husband and wife. They lived together for some twenty years, until his death in 1878. Two years after Lewes's death, Mary Ann married a man twenty years younger than her. Seven months after she married, however, she died of a throat infection.

Despite Mary Ann's scandalous love life, her first novel, *Adam Bede*, was published in 1859 and was a bestseller. The identity of the author was the subject of much speculation and, because *Adam Bede* was so popular, Mary Ann made it known that she was the author. If her readers didn't approve of her personal life, they didn't show it. They wanted to read her books. She went on to write six more novels, most of which were instant hits. With the publication of *Middlemarch*, she claimed her place in England as one of the country's most important writers.

From *Middlemarch*

Miss Brooke had that kind of beauty which seems to be thrown into relief by poor dress. Her hand and wrist were so finely formed that she could wear sleeves not less bare of style than those in which the Blessed Virgin appeared to Italian painters; and her profile as well as her stature and bearing seemed to gain the more dignity from her plain garments, which by the side of provincial fashion gave her the impressiveness of a fine quotation from the Bible,—or from one of our elder poets,—in a paragraph of to-day's newspaper. She was usually spoken of as being remarkably clever, but with the addition that her sister Celia had more common-sense.

* * *

Her mind was theoretic, and yearned by its nature after some lofty conception of the world which might frankly include the parish of Tipton and her own rule of conduct there; she was enamoured of intensity and greatness, and rash in embracing whatever seemed to her to have those aspects; likely to seek martyrdom, to make retractations, and then to incur martyrdom after all in a quarter where she had not sought it. Certainly such elements in the character of a marriageable girl tended to interfere with her lot, and hinder it from being decided according to custom, by good looks, vanity, and merely canine affection.

* * *

And how should Dorothea not marry?—a girl so handsome and with such prospects? Nothing could hinder it but her love of extremes, and her insistence on regulating life according to notions which might cause a wary man to hesitate before he made her an offer, or even might lead her at last to refuse all offers. A young lady of some birth and fortune, who knelt suddenly down on a brick floor by the side of a sick laborer and prayed fervidly as if she thought herself living in the time of the Apostles—who had strange whims of fasting like a Papist, and of sitting up at night to read old theological books! Such a wife might awaken you some fine morning with a new scheme for the application of her income which would interfere with political economy and the keeping of saddle-horses: a man would naturally think twice before he risked himself in such fellowship. Women were expected to have weak opinions; but the great safeguard of society and of domestic life was, that opinions were not acted on. Sane people did what their neighbors did, so that if any lunatics were at large, one might know and avoid them.

The rural opinion about the new young ladies, even among the cottagers, was generally in favor of Celia, as being so amiable and innocent-looking, while Miss Brooke's large eyes seemed, like her religion, too unusual and striking. Poor Dorothea! compared with her, the innocent-looking Celia was knowing and worldly-wise; so much subtler is a human mind than the outside tissues which make a sort of blazonry or clock-face for it.

Yet those who approached Dorothea, though prejudiced against her by this alarming hearsay, found that she had a charm unaccountably reconcilable with it. Most men thought her bewitching when she was on horseback. She loved the fresh air and the various aspects of the country, and when her eyes and cheeks glowed with mingled pleasure she looked very little like a devotee. Riding was an indulgence which she allowed herself in spite of conscientious qualms; she felt that she enjoyed it in a pagan sensuous way, and always looked forward to renouncing it.

Novel Knowledge: ELIOT POKES FUN AT CHICK LIT

Eliot wrote an essay for the *Westminster Review* titled "Silly Novels by Lady Novelists." The essay poked fun at the ridiculous and petty story lines in books written by women at the time.

She was open, ardent, and not in the least self-admiring; indeed, it was pretty to see how her imagination adorned her sister Celia with attractions altogether superior to her own, and if any gentleman appeared to come to the Grange from some other motive than that of seeing Mr. Brooke, she concluded that he must be in love with Celia: Sir James Chettam, for example, whom she constantly considered from Celia's point of view, inwardly debating whether it would be good for Celia to accept him. That he should be regarded as a suitor to herself would have seemed to her a ridiculous irrelevance. Dorothea, with all her eagerness to know the truths of life, retained very childlike ideas about marriage. She felt sure that she would have accepted the judicious Hooker, if she had been born in time to save him from that wretched mistake he made in matrimony; or John Milton when his blindness had come on; or any of the other great men whose odd habits it would have been glorious piety to endure; but an amiable handsome baronet, who said "Exactly" to her remarks even when she expressed uncertainty,—how could he affect her as a lover? The really delightful marriage must be that where your husband was a sort of father, and could teach you even Hebrew, if you wished it.

* * *

Mr. Brooke sat down in his arm-chair, stretched his legs towards the wood-fire, which had fallen into a wondrous mass of glowing dice between the dogs, and rubbed his hands gently, looking very mildly towards Dorothea, but with a neutral leisurely air, as if he had nothing particular to say. Dorothea closed her pamphlet, as soon as she was aware of her uncle's presence, and rose as if to go. Usually she would have been interested about her uncle's merciful errand on behalf of the criminal, but her late agitation had made her absent-minded.

* * *

"You like him, eh?" said Mr. Brooke, without showing any surprise, or other emotion. "Well, now, I've known Casaubon ten years, ever since he came to Lowick. But I never got anything out of him—any ideas, you know. However, he is a tiptop man and may be a bishop—that kind of thing, you know, if Peel stays in. And he has a very high opinion of you, my dear."

Dorothea could not speak.

"The fact is, he has a very high opinion indeed of you. And he speaks uncommonly well—does Casaubon. He has deferred to me, you not being of age. In short, I have promised to speak to you, though I told him I thought there was not much chance. I was bound to tell him that. I said, my niece is very young, and that kind of thing. But I didn't think it necessary to go into everything. However, the long and the short of it is, that he has asked my permission to make you an offer of marriage—of marriage, you know," said Mr. Brooke, with his explanatory nod. "I thought it better to tell you, my dear."

No one could have detected any anxiety in Mr. Brooke's manner, but he did really wish to know something of his niece's mind, that, if there were any need for advice, he might give it in time. What feeling he, as a magistrate who had taken in so many ideas, could make room for, was unmixedly kind. Since Dorothea did not speak immediately, he repeated, "I thought it better to tell you, my dear."

"Thank you, uncle," said Dorothea, in a clear unwavering tone. "I am very grateful to Mr. Casaubon. If he makes me an offer, I shall accept him. I admire and honor him more than any man I ever saw."

Novel Knowledge: A Big Fan

Virginia Woolf, a fan of George Eliot's work, described *Middlemarch* as "one of the few English novels written for grown-up people."

Mr. Brooke paused a little, and then said in a lingering low tone, "Ah? . . . Well! He is a good match in some respects. But now, Chettam is a good match. And our land lies together. I shall never interfere against your wishes, my dear. People should have their own way in marriage, and that sort of thing—up to a certain point, you know. I have always said that, up to a certain point.

I wish you to marry well; and I have good reason to believe that Chettam wishes to marry you. I mention it, you know."

"It is impossible that I should ever marry Sir James Chettam," said Dorothea. "If he thinks of marrying me, he has made a great mistake."

"That is it, you see. One never knows. I should have thought Chettam was just the sort of man a woman would like, now."

"Pray do not mention him in that light again, uncle," said Dorothea, feeling some of her late irritation revive.

Mr. Brooke wondered, and felt that women were an inexhaustible subject of study, since even he at his age was not in a perfect state of scientific prediction about them. Here was a fellow like Chettam with no chance at all.

"Well, but Casaubon, now. There is no hurry—I mean for you. It's true, every year will tell upon him. He is over five-and-forty, you know. I should say a good seven-and-twenty years older than you. To be sure,—if you like learning and standing, and that sort of thing, we can't have everything. And his income is good—he has a handsome property independent of the Church—his income is good. Still he is not young, and I must not conceal from you, my dear, that I think his health is not over-strong. I know nothing else against him."

"I should not wish to have a husband very near my own age," said Dorothea, with grave decision. "I should wish to have a husband who was above me in judgment and in all knowledge."

Mr. Brooke repeated his subdued, "Ah?—I thought you had more of your own opinion than most girls. I thought you liked your own opinion—liked it, you know."

"I cannot imagine myself living without some opinions, but I should wish to have good reasons for them, and a wise man could help me to see which opinions had the best foundation, and would help me to live according to them."

"Very true. You couldn't put the thing better—couldn't put it better, beforehand, you know. But there are oddities in things," continued Mr. Brooke, whose conscience was really roused to do the best he could for his niece on this occasion. "Life isn't cast in a mould—not cut out by rule and line, and that sort of thing. I never married myself, and it will be the better for you and yours. The fact is, I never loved any one well enough to put myself into a noose for them. It is a noose, you know. Temper, now. There is temper. And a husband likes to be master."

"I know that I must expect trials, uncle. Marriage is a state of higher duties. I never thought of it as mere personal ease," said poor Dorothea.

"Well, you are not fond of show, a great establishment, balls, dinners, that kind of thing. I can see that Casaubon's ways might suit you better than Chettam's. And you shall do as you like, my dear. I would not hinder Casaubon; I said so at once; for there is no knowing how anything may turn out. You have not the same tastes as every young lady; and a clergyman and scholar—who may be a bishop—that kind of thing—may suit you better than Chettam. Chettam is a good fellow, a good sound-hearted fellow, you know; but he doesn't go much into ideas. I did, when I was his age. But Casaubon's eyes, now. I think he has hurt them a little with too much reading."

"I should be all the happier, uncle, the more room there was for me to help him," said Dorothea, ardently.

"You have quite made up your mind, I see. Well, my dear, the fact is, I have a letter for you in my pocket." Mr. Brooke handed the letter to Dorothea, but as she rose to go away, he added, "There is not too much hurry, my dear. Think about it, you know."

When Dorothea had left him, he reflected that he had certainly spoken strongly: he had put the risks of marriage before her in a striking manner. It was his duty to do so. But as to pretending to be wise for young people,—no uncle, however much he had travelled in his youth, absorbed the new ideas, and dined with celebrities now deceased, could pretend to judge what sort of marriage would turn out well for a young girl who preferred Casaubon to Chettam. In short, woman was a problem which, since Mr. Brooke's mind felt blank before it, could be hardly less complicated than the revolutions of an irregular solid.

Tita de la Garza

IN *LIKE WATER FOR CHOCOLATE* BY LAURA ESQUIVEL
FIRST PUBLISHED IN: 1989

Who is she? A passionate woman who celebrates and laments through cooking.

Her Story

Tita de la Garza is passionate about two things: Food and Pedro. She brings a lot of joy to a lot of people with her cooking, and Pedro brings her more joy than she ever imagined a man could.

Unfortunately for Tita, her mother, Mama Elena, takes a long-standing family tradition very seriously. According to the tradition, Tita cannot marry and, as the youngest daughter, is instead expected to take care of her aging mother. As if that isn't bad enough, Mama Elena takes matters a step further and suggests that Pedro marry Rosaura, the middle daughter, since she is available. Pedro, broken-hearted, sees this as his only way to stay near Tita and agrees to marry Rosaura instead. Devastated by Pedro's decision, Tita is left with only one passion—food.

Once Pedro marries Rosaura, however, the dishes Tita prepares have a strange, mystical effect on people. From sexual desires to uncontrollable tears, Tita's own passionate feelings seep into the mixing bowl. Anyone who tastes Tita's cooking experiences her emotions and desires. Years later this mystical effect overwhelms Pedro and Tita and they finally make love. Tita fears she may be pregnant, but she also begins to realize that she is a strong woman who can handle anything fate decides to send her way.

What Makes Tita de la Garza So Memorable?

Tita is a passionate young woman who celebrates and laments through cooking. She expresses her patience and care when kneading and rolling out dough and she shows love in the way she prepares her Christmas rolls and cream fritters. Tita understands precisely how much cumin and sugar she needs to make a delicious *champandongo* and she always takes the time to prepare her dishes exactly as they should be prepared. Even more, she tries to improve her life and the world around her through her cooking. And just as her Christmas rolls leave a lasting impression on the palate, Tita leaves a lasting impression on anyone who sits at her table.

The Life and Times of Laura Esquivel

Laura Esquivel began writing while teaching kindergarten. She wrote plays for children, then went on to write children's television programs. *Like Water for Chocolate* was her debut novel. Since then she has written *Law of Love*, *Between the Fires*, and, most recently, *Malinche*. She married and later divorced actor-director Alfonso Arau. Active in political issues, she ran and lost a bid for a Mexican congressional seat in 2009. Esquivel lives in Mexico City, Mexico.

FROM *Like Water for Chocolate*

Tita's domain was the kitchen, where she grew vigorous and healthy on a diet of teas and thin corn gruels. This explains the sixth sense Tita developed about everything concerning food. Her eating habits, for example, were attuned to the kitchen routine: in the morning, when she could smell that the beans were ready; at midday, when she sensed the water was ready for plucking the chickens; and in the afternoon, when the dinner bread was baking, Tita knew it was time for her to be fed.

Sometimes she would cry for no reason at all, like when Nacha chopped onions, but since they both knew the cause of those tears, they didn't pay them much mind. They made them a source of entertainment, so that during her childhood Tita didn't distinguish between tears of laughter and tears of sorrow. For her laughing was a form of crying.

Novel Knowledge: WHAT DOES IT MEAN?

The saying "like water for chocolate" refers to the Mexican tradition of using water rather than milk when making hot chocolate. The expression in Spanish, "como agua para chocolate," has a double meaning. It can mean something similar to the American phrase "boiling mad," or it can also refer to sexual passion.

Likewise for Tita the joy of living was wrapped up in the delights of food. It wasn't easy for a person whose knowledge of life was based on the kitchen to comprehend the outside world. That world was an endless expanse that began at the door between the kitchen and the rest of the house, whereas everything on the kitchen side of that door, on through the door leading to the patio and the kitchen and herb gardens was completely hers—it was Tita's realm.

Her sisters were just the opposite: to them, Tita's world seemed full of unknown dangers, and they were terrified of it. They felt that playing in the kitchen was foolish and dangerous. But once, Tita managed to convince them to join her in watching the dazzling display made by dancing water drops dribbled on a red hot griddle.

While Tita was singing and waving her wet hands in time, showering drops of water down on the griddle so they would "dance," Rosaura was cowering in the corner, stunned by the display. Gertrudis, on the other hand, found this game enticing, and she threw herself into it with the enthusiasm she always showed where rhythm, movement, or music were involved. Then Rosaura had tried to join them—but since she barely moistened her hands and then shook them gingerly, her efforts didn't have the desired effect. So Tita tried to move her hands closer to the griddle. Rosaura resisted, and they struggled for control until Tita became annoyed and let go, so that momentum carried Rosaura's hands onto it. Tita got a terrible spanking for that, and she was forbidden to play with her sisters in her own world. Nacha became her playmate then. Together they made up all sorts of games and activities having to do with cooking. Like the day they saw a man in the village plaza twisting long thin balloons into animal shapes, and they decided to do it with sausages. They didn't just make real animals, they also made up some of their own, creatures with the neck of a swan, the legs of a dog, the tail of a horse, and on and on.

Then there was trouble, however, when the animals had to be taken apart to fry the sausage. Tita refused to do it. The only time she was willing to take them apart was when the sausage was intended for the Christmas rolls she loved so much. Then she not only allowed her animals to be dismantled, she watched them fry with glee.

The sausage for the rolls must be fried over very low heat, so that it cooks thoroughly without getting too brown. When done, remove from the heat and add the sardines, which have been deboned ahead of time. Any black spots on the skin should also have been scraped off with a knife. Combine the onions, chopped chiles, and the ground oregano with the sardines. Let the mixture stand before filling the rolls.

Tita enjoyed this step enormously; while the filling was resting, it was very pleasant to savor its aroma, for smells have the power to evoke the past, bringing back sounds and even other smells that have no match in the present. Tita liked to take a deep breath and let the characteristic smoke and smell transport her through the recesses of her memory.

Novel Knowledge: FAVORITE RECIPES

For those who have read the book and tried the recipes, the Northern Style Chorizo (Chapter 5) and the Quail in Rose Petal Sauce (Chapter 3) seem to be among the favorites.

It was useless to try to recall the first time she had smelled one of those rolls—she couldn't, possibly because it had been before she was born. It might have been the unusual combination of sardines and sausages that had called to her and made her decide to trade the peace of ethereal existence in Mama Elena's belly for life as her daughter, in order to enter the De la Garza family and share their delicious meals and wonderful sausage.

* * *

As soon as the sergeant was gone, Tita lay down on her bed again. She had no desire to be anywhere else; her belly was too swollen, and she couldn't sit for very long.

Tita thought of the many times she had germinated kernels or seeds of rice, beans, or alfalfa, without giving any thought to how it felt for them to grow and change form so radically. Now she admired the way they opened their skin and allowed the water to penetrate them fully, until they were split asunder to make way for new life. She imagined the pride they felt as the tip of the first root emerged from inside of them, the humility with which they accepted the loss of their previous form, the bravery with which they showed the world their new leaves. Tita would love to be a simple seed, not to have to explain to anyone what was growing inside her, to show her fertile belly to the world without laying herself open to society's disapproval. Seeds didn't have that kind of problem, they didn't have a mother to be afraid of or a fear of those who would judge them. Tita no longer had a mother but she couldn't get rid of the feeling that any minute some awful punishment was going to descend on her from the great beyond, courtesy of Mama Elena. That was a familiar feeling; it was like the fear she felt when she was cooking and didn't follow a recipe to the letter. She was always sure when she did it that Mama Elena would find out and, instead of congratulating her on her creativity, give her a terrible tongue-lashing for disobeying the rules. But she couldn't resist the temptation to violate the oh-so-rigid rules her mother imposed in the kitchen . . . and in life.

From *Like Water for Chocolate* by Laura Esquivel. Copyright © translation 1992 by Doubleday, a div. of Random House, Inc. Used by permission of Doubleday, a division of Random House, Inc.

Gloria Patch

IN *THE BEAUTIFUL AND THE DAMNED*
BY F. SCOTT FITZGERALD
FIRST PUBLISHED IN: 1922

Who is she? A woman who imagines she will be young forever.

Her Story

Gloria is naive, spoiled, and remarkably sure of herself. Anthony Patch is financially set for life. The two know little else about themselves—or each other—when they fall in love, marry, and together decide to "do nothing." As far as they're concerned, there's nothing "that's worth doing." Instead, they prefer to wait for Anthony's grandfather to die so Anthony can take over the family estate. In the meantime, they go about town looking dapper and lovely. When they aren't giving lavish parties, they attend them. And they live large . . . too large.

Unfortunately for them, Anthony's grandfather lives to be a very old man, and Anthony's trust fund dries up. People stop inviting the glamorous couple to parties. Even more, old friends move on with their lives. They have careers, children, and responsibilities while Gloria and Anthony do everything they can to avoid growing up. Then, when Anthony's grandfather finally dies, he leaves them nothing. Gloria finally understands that she needs more than her good looks to get by in the world. And so, the fight for time and money is on. As it turns out, Gloria is much more of a fighter than her husband. She's much more of a fighter than she ever imagined.

What Makes Gloria Patch So Memorable?

Gloria Patch is both naive and abrasive, soft and selfish. She is smart, but prefers not to think. Beautiful but ignorant of the tricks time plays on one's looks. She is a stark reminder of what happens when a woman relies too heavily on her beauty. Her crash into a penniless world, shell-shocked and angry, is also a reminder that anyone can fall on hard times. Soon after the book's release, Gloria's experience was shared by women, hard-working or well-to-do all across the country. Her determination, though of a selfish nature, and her unexpected courage are heartening, especially in tough times.

The Life and Times of F. Scott Fitzgerald

F. Scott Fitzgerald was born in St. Paul, Minnesota, in 1896. He met Zelda Sayre in 1919 while stationed at the Military Camp Sheridan near Montgomery, Alabama. She was the beautiful daughter of a State Supreme Court Judge and Fitzgerald couldn't stand the thought of life without her. He asked her to marry him, but Zelda was worried that a writer wouldn't be able to support the lifestyle she was accustomed to living. Eventually, though, she said yes and the couple married and lived together in New York. Fitzgerald worked for an advertising firm, wrote short stories, and completed his first novel, *This Side of Paradise*. The novel was published in 1920 and became a bestseller that same year. Fitzgerald followed up this success with his novel *The Beautiful and the Damned*.

In 1921, soon after their only child, Scottie, was born, Zelda was diagnosed with schizophrenia. Despite her emotional frailty, and unpredictability, Fitzgerald was devoted to Zelda's happiness and health. After her first breakdown in 1930, Fitzgerald wrote frantically in order to make money and pay for her lengthy stays in mental hospitals. He would have preferred to spend more time writing novels, but money came faster with short stories, so for the sake of Zelda's health, and their standard of living, he wrote for magazines and earned money as quickly as possible.

He wrote his greatest literary achievement, *The Great Gatsby*, in 1925, but the novel didn't make him nearly as much money as his earlier works and, in the late 1930s, he moved to California to write for the big screen. He hated the work, but it paid well. He began writing *The Last Tycoon* while there. It was to be his final novel. Though he continued to care for and write letters to Zelda, he saw very little of her. She moved into a mental institution while he stayed in California. In December of 1940, Fitzgerald died of a massive heart attack. Eight years later, while Zelda was living at the Highland Hospital in Asheville, North Carolina, a fire broke out. She was one of nine women to die in the blaze.

From *The Beautiful and the Damned*

It was with this party, more especially with Gloria's part in it, that a decided change began to come over their way of living. The magnificent attitude of not giving a damn altered over-night; from being a mere tenet of Gloria's it became the entire solace and justification for what they chose to do and what consequence it brought. Not to be sorry, not to loose one cry of regret, to live according to a clear code of honor toward each other, and to seek the moment's happiness as fervently and persistently as possible.

"No one cares about us but ourselves, Anthony," she said one day. "It'd be ridiculous for me to go about pretending I felt any obligations toward the world, and as for worrying what people think about me, I simply *don't*, that's all. Since I was a little girl in dancing-school I've been criticized by the mothers of all the little girls who weren't as popular as I was, and I've always looked on criticism as a sort of envious tribute."

This was because of a party in the "Boul' Mich'" one night, where Constance Merriam had seen her as one of a highly stimulated party of four. Constance Merriam, "as an old school friend," had gone to the trouble of inviting her to lunch next day in order to inform her how terrible it was.

"I told her I couldn't see it," Gloria told Anthony. "Eric Merriam is a sort of sublimated Percy Wolcott—you remember that man in Hot Springs I told you about—his idea of respecting Constance is to leave her at home with her sewing and her baby and her book, and such innocuous amusements, whenever he's going on a party that promises to be anything but deathly dull."

"Did you tell her that?"

"I certainly did. And I told her that what she really objected to was that I was having a better time than she was."

Anthony applauded her. He was tremendously proud of Gloria, proud that she never failed to eclipse whatever other women might be in the party, proud that men were always glad to revel with her in great rowdy groups, without any attempt to do more than enjoy her beauty and the warmth of her vitality.

These "parties" gradually became their chief source of entertainment. Still in love, still enormously interested in each other, they yet found as spring drew near that staying at home in the evening palled on them; books were unreal; the old magic of being alone had long since vanished—instead they preferred to be bored by a stupid musical comedy, or to go to dinner with the most uninteresting of their acquaintances, so long as there would be enough cocktails to keep the conversation from becoming utterly intolerable. A scattering of younger married people who had been their friends in school or college, as well as a varied assortment of single men, began to think instinctively of them whenever color and excitement were needed, so there was scarcely a day without its phone call, its "Wondered what you were doing this evening." Wives, as a rule, were afraid of Gloria—her facile attainment of the centre of the stage, her innocent but nevertheless disturbing way of becoming a favorite with husbands—these things drove them instinctively into an attitude of profound distrust, heightened by the fact that Gloria was largely unresponsive to any intimacy shown her by a woman.

Novel Knowledge: FITZGERALD AND THE MOVIES

The film version of *Gone with the Wind* was among the movies Fitzgerald worked on while in Hollywood. Unfortunately, his writing on the film was not used in the final version.

On the appointed Wednesday in February Anthony had gone to the imposing offices of Wilson, Hiemer and Hardy and listened to many vague instructions delivered by an energetic young man of about his own age, named Kahler, who wore a defiant yellow pompadour, and in announcing himself as an assistant secretary gave the impression that it was a tribute to exceptional ability.

"There's two kinds of men here, you'll find," he said. "There's the man who gets to be an assistant secretary or treasurer, gets his name on our folder here, before he's thirty, and there's the man who gets his hand there at forty-five. The man who gets his name there at forty-five stays there the rest of his life."

"How about the man who gets it there at thirty?" inquired Anthony politely.

"Why, he gets up here, you see." He pointed to a list of assistant vice-presidents upon the folder. "Or maybe he gets to be president or secretary or treasurer."

"And what about these over here?"

"Those? Oh, those are the trustees—the men with capital."

"I see."

"Now some people," continued Kahler, "think that whether a man gets started early or late depends on whether he's got a college education. But they're wrong."

"I see."

"I had one; I was Buckleigh, class of nineteen-eleven, but when I came down to the Street I soon found that the things that would help me here weren't the fancy things that I learned in college. In fact, I had to get a lot of fancy stuff out of my head."

Anthony could not help wondering what possible "fancy stuff" he had learned at Buckleigh in nineteen-eleven. An irrepressible idea that it was some sort of needlework recurred to him throughout the rest of the conversation.

"See that fellow over there?" Kahler pointed to a youngish-looking man with handsome gray hair, sitting at a desk inside a mahogany railing. "That's Mr. Ellinger, the first vice-president. Been everywhere, seen everything; got a fine education."

In vain did Anthony try to open his mind to the romance of finance; he could think of Mr. Ellinger only as one of the buyers of the handsome leather sets of Thackeray, Balzac, Hugo, and Gibbon that lined the walls of the big bookstores.

Through the damp and uninspiring month of March he was prepared for salesmanship. Lacking enthusiasm he was capable of viewing the turmoil and bustle that surrounded him only as a fruitless circumambient striving toward an incomprehensible goal, tangibly evidenced only by the rival mansions of Mr. Frick and Mr. Carnegie on Fifth Avenue. That these portentous vice-presidents and trustees should be actually the fathers of the "best men" he had known at Harvard seemed to him incongruous.

Novel Knowledge: THE OTHER F. SCOTT

Francis Scott Key, author of the "Star-Spangled Banner," was Francis Scott Fitzgerald's namesake and second cousin, three times removed on his mother's side.

He ate in an employees' lunch-room up-stairs with an uneasy suspicion that he was being uplifted, wondering through that first week if the dozens of young clerks, some of them alert and immaculate, and just out of college, lived in flamboyant hope of crowding onto that narrow slip of cardboard before the catastrophic thirties. The conversation that interwove with the pattern of the day's work was all much of a piece. One discussed how Mr. Wilson had made his money, what method Mr. Heimer had employed, and the means resorted to by Mr. Hardy. One related age-old but eternally breathless anecdotes of the fortunes stumbled on precipitously in the Street by a "butcher" or a "bartender," or "a darn messenger boy, by golly!" and then one talked of the current gambles, and whether it was best to go out for a hundred thousand a year or be content with twenty. During the preceding year one of the assistant secretaries had invested all his savings in Bethlehem Steel. The story of his spectacular magnificence, of his haughty resignations in January, and of the triumphal palace he was now building in California, was the favorite office subject. The man's very name had acquired a magic significance, symbolizing as he did the aspirations of all good Americans. Anecdotes were told about him—how one of the vice-presidents had advised him to sell, by golly, but he had hung on, even bought on margin, "and *now* look where he is!"

Such, obviously, was the stuff of life—a dizzy triumph dazzling the eyes of all of them, a gypsy siren to content them with meagre wage and with the arithmetical improbability of their eventual success.

To Anthony the notion became appalling. He felt that to succeed here the idea of success must grasp and limit his mind. It seemed to him that the essential element in these men at the top was their faith that their affairs were the very core of life. All other things being equal, self-assurance and opportunism won out over technical knowledge; it was obvious that the more expert work went on near the bottom—so, with appropriate efficiency, the technical experts were kept there.

His determination to stay in at night during the week did not survive, and a good half of the time he came to work with a splitting, sickish headache and the crowded horror of the morning subway ringing in his ears like an echo of hell.

Then, abruptly, he quit. He had remained in bed all one Monday, and late in the evening, overcome by one of those attacks of moody despair to which he periodically succumbed, he wrote and mailed a letter to Mr. Wilson, confessing that he considered himself ill adapted to the work. Gloria, coming in from the theatre with Richard Caramel, found him on the lounge, silently staring at the high ceiling, more depressed and discouraged than he had been at any time since their marriage.

She wanted him to whine. If he had she would have reproached him bitterly, for she was not a little annoyed, but he only lay there so utterly miserable that she felt sorry for him, and kneeling down she stroked his head, saying how little it mattered, how little anything mattered so long as they loved each other. It was like their first year, and Anthony, reacting to her cool hand, to her voice that was soft as breath itself upon his ear, became almost cheerful, and talked with her of his future plans. He even regretted, silently, before he went to bed that he had so hastily mailed his resignation.

"Even when everything seems rotten you can't trust that judgment," Gloria had said. "It's the sum of all your judgments that counts."

Tess Durbeyfield

IN *TESS OF THE D'URBERVILLES* BY THOMAS HARDY

FIRST PUBLISHED IN: 1891

Who is she? An innocent young woman caught up in Victorian double standards.

Her Story

Tess Durbeyfield wants a simple life near her family, but she lives during a time when a woman's future depends completely on the man she marries. Though beautiful, Tess's chances of marrying a good man quickly fade when her father insists that she live with their newfound wealthy relatives, the d'Urbervilles. Tess's situation there goes from bad to worse when Alec, the spoiled son of the noble d'Urbervilles, tries to seduce his naive cousin. Frightened by his advances and intimidated by his money, Tess reluctantly becomes his mistress. She is miserable with her new way of life. Even more, she is pregnant. She returns home without telling Alec about the baby only to find that even her father is now ashamed of her.

The baby dies soon after birth, and Tess goes to work on a dairy farm where she meets Angel Clare. With Angel, she hopes to put her sad, sordid past out of her mind; though she wants to come clean about Alec and the baby. On their wedding night, Angel confesses his liaison with a woman in London before he and Tess met. Tess forgives him and, expecting the same in return, reveals her dark secret. Angel is devastated and can't find it in his heart to forgive his new bride. "O Tess, forgiveness does not apply to the case! You were one person; now you are another. My God—how can forgiveness meet such a grotesque—prestidigitation as that!"

Angel leaves Tess and goes to Brazil. At first, Tess hopes that he'll forgive her and come back. But as time passes and he doesn't respond to her letters, she grows cold and angry. Heartbroken and full of rage, she writes to him one final letter. "O why have you treated me so monstrously, Angel! I do not deserve it. I have thought it all over carefully, and I can never, never forgive you! You know that I did not intend to wrong you— why have you so wronged me? You are cruel, cruel indeed! I will try to forget you. It is all injustice I have received at your hands!"

Novel Knowledge: CENSORED

Tess of the d'Urbervilles was censored (due to its sexuality) when first published in a serialized format in *The Graphic,* a British illustrated paper.

No longer naive and certainly not easily frightened nor intimated by men, Tess comes into her own. She is a strong woman and takes full credit or suffers all the consequences for any decisions she makes. There is peace in knowing the decisions are her own. There is peace is knowing that she doesn't belong to anyone. Or does she? Can a woman in Victorian times ever be independent of a man? If so, it certainly isn't easy. But Tess understands that and doesn't expect anything to come easy.

What Makes Tess Durbeyfield So Memorable?

Tess Durbeyfield's life reveals what happens when a good woman is forced to depend on men for everything. As a victim of Victorian double standards, she is easy to sympathize with. However, once she is pushed to the edge, she begins to challenge the expectations society places on women. In a moment of anger and frustration, she takes control of her own life. In doing so, she learns the peace of mind that comes with controlling one's own destiny—if only for a short time.

The Life and Times of Thomas Hardy

For most of his life, Thomas Hardy was a well-known, award-winning architect. But he had a knack for writing poems and in his later years enjoyed a successful and respected writing career. He published his first set of poetry in his fifties before he began to write novels. Born in Dorset, England, in 1840, Hardy was keenly aware of social class and his own low ranking by society's standards.

In 1874, he fell in love with and married Emma Lavinia Gifford. When she died in 1912, Hardy was deeply affected. His collection titled *Poems 1912–13* focuses on her death and her absence from his life. Hardy remarried two years after Emma died, but he kept writing poetry about his first wife.

When Hardy died in 1928, his family arranged for him to be buried at St. Michael's Church in Stinsford alongside Emma, yet his literary contributions permitted, almost demanded, that he be buried at Poet's Corner in Westminster Abbey. In an unusual compromise, the family agreed to let his ashes rest at Westminster and his heart be buried at Stinsford.

From *Tess of the d'Urbervilles*

They came round by The Pure Drop Inn, and were turning out of the high road to pass through a wicket-gate into the meadows, when one of the women said—

"The Load-a-Lord! Why, Tess Durbeyfield, if there isn't thy father riding home in a carriage!"

A young member of the band turned her head at the exclamation. She was a fine and handsome girl—not handsomer than some others, possibly—but her mobile peony mouth and large innocent eyes added eloquence to colour and shape. She wore a red ribbon in her hair, and was the only one of the white company who could boast of such a pronounced adornment. As she looked round Durbeyfield was seen moving along the road in a chaise belonging to The Pure Drop, driven by a frizzle-headed brawny damsel with her gown-sleeves rolled above her elbows. This was the cheerful servant of that establishment, who, in her part of factotum, turned groom and ostler at times.

Durbeyfield, leaning back, and with his eyes closed luxuriously, was waving his hand above his head, and singing in a slow recitative—

"I've-got-a-gr't-family-vault-at-Kingsbere—and knighted-forefathers-in-lead-coffins-there!"

The clubbists tittered, except the girl called Tess—in whom a slow heat seemed to rise at the sense that her father was making himself foolish in their eyes.

"He's tired, that's all," she said hastily, "and he has got a lift home, because our own horse has to rest to-day."

"Bless thy simplicity, Tess," said her companions. "He's got his market-nitch. Haw-haw!"

"Look here; I won't walk another inch with you, if you say any jokes about him!" Tess cried, and the colour upon her cheeks spread over her face and neck. In a moment her eyes grew moist, and her glance drooped to the ground. Perceiving that they had really pained her they said no more, and order again prevailed. Tess's pride would not allow her to turn her head again, to learn what her father's meaning was, if he had any; and thus she moved on with the whole body to the enclosure where there was to be dancing on the green. By the time the spot was reached she has recovered her equanimity, and tapped her neighbour with her wand and talked as usual.

Tess Durbeyfield at this time of her life was a mere vessel of emotion untinctured by experience. The dialect was on her tongue to some extent, despite the village school: the characteristic intonation of that dialect for this district being the voicing approximately rendered by the syllable UR, probably as rich an utterance as any to be found in human speech. The pouted-up deep red mouth to which this syllable was native had hardly as yet settled into its definite shape, and her lower lip had a way of thrusting the middle of her top one upward, when they closed together after a word.

Phases of her childhood lurked in her aspect still. As she walked along to-day, for all her bouncing handsome womanliness, you could sometimes see her twelfth year in her cheeks, or her ninth sparkling from her eyes; and even her fifth would flit over the curves of her mouth now and then.

Yet few knew, and still fewer considered this. A small minority, mainly strangers, would look long at her in casually passing by, and grow momentarily fascinated by her freshness, and wonder if they would ever see her again: but to almost everybody she was a fine and picturesque country girl, and no more.

Nothing was seen or heard further of Durbeyfield in his triumphal chariot under the conduct of the ostleress, and the club having entered the allotted space, dancing began. As there were no men in the company, the girls danced at first with each other, but when the hour for the close of labour drew on, the masculine inhabitants of the village, together with other idlers and pedestrians, gathered round the spot, and appeared inclined to negotiate for a partner.

Among these on-lookers were three young men of a superior class, carrying small knapsacks strapped to their shoulders, and stout sticks in their hands. Their general likeness to each other, and their consecutive ages, would almost have suggested that they might be, what in fact they were, brothers. The eldest wore the white tie, high waistcoat, and thin-brimmed hat of the regulation curate; the second was the normal undergraduate; the appearance of the third and youngest would hardly have been sufficient to characterize him; there was an uncribbed, uncabined aspect in his eyes and attire, implying that he had hardly as yet found the entrance to his professional groove. That he was a desultory tentative student of something and everything might only have been predicted of him.

These three brethren told casual acquaintance that they were spending their Whitsun holidays in a walking tour through the Vale of Blackmoor, their course being south-westerly from the town of Shaston on the north-east.

They leant over the gate by the highway, and inquired as to the meaning of the dance and the white-frocked maids. The two elder of the brothers were plainly not intending to linger more than a moment, but the spectacle of a bevy of girls dancing without male partners seemed to amuse the third, and make him in no hurry to move on. He unstrapped his knapsack, put it, with his stick, on the hedge-bank, and opened the gate.

"What are you going to do, Angel?" asked the eldest.

"I am inclined to go and have a fling with them. Why not all of us—just for a minute or two—it will not detain us long?"

"No—no; nonsense!" said the first. "Dancing in public with a troop of country hoydens—suppose we should be seen! Come along, or it will be dark before we get to Stourcastle, and there's no place we can sleep at nearer than that; besides, we must get through another chapter of *A Counterblast to Agnosticism* before we turn in, now I have taken the trouble to bring the book."

"All right—I'll overtake you and Cuthbert in five minutes; don't stop; I give my word that I will, Felix."

The two elder reluctantly left him and walked on, taking their brother's knapsack to relieve him in following, and the youngest entered the field.

"This is a thousand pities," he said gallantly, to two or three of the girls nearest him, as soon as there was a pause in the dance. "Where are your partners, my dears?"

"They've not left off work yet," answered one of the boldest. "They'll be here by and by. Till then, will you be one, sir?"

"Certainly. But what's one among so many!"

"Better than none. 'Tis melancholy work facing and footing it to one of your own sort, and no clipsing and colling at all. Now, pick and choose."

"Ssh—don't be so for'ard!" said a shyer girl.

The young man, thus invited, glanced them over, and attempted some discrimination; but, as the group were all so new to him, he could not very well exercise it. He took almost the first that came to hand, which was not the speaker, as she had expected; nor did it happen to be Tess Durbeyfield. Pedigree, ancestral skeletons, monumental record, the d'Urberville lineaments, did not help Tess in her life's battle as yet, even to the extent of attracting to her a dancing-partner over the heads of the commonest peasantry. So much for Norman blood unaided by Victorian lucre.

Novel Knowledge: THE CLIFFHANGER

Thomas Hardy created the writing technique that leaves a reader in suspense at the end of a story or chapter. This was first done when he wrote his novel *A Pair of Blue Eyes.* In the story, which was serialized from 1872 to 1873, one of the main characters is literally left dangling from a cliff at the end of a chapter. Readers loved it.

The name of the eclipsing girl, whatever it was, has not been handed down; but she was envied by all as the first who enjoyed the luxury of a masculine partner that evening. Yet such was the force of example that the village young men, who had not hastened to enter the gate while no intruder was in the way, now dropped in quickly, and soon the couples became leavened with rustic youth to a marked extent, till at length the plainest woman in the club was no longer compelled to foot it on the masculine side of the figure.

The church clock struck, when suddenly the student said that he must leave—he had been forgetting himself—he had to join his companions. As he fell out of the dance his eyes lighted on Tess Durbeyfield, whose own large orbs wore, to tell the truth, the faintest aspect of reproach that he had not chosen her. He, too, was sorry then that, owing to her backwardness, he had not observed her; and with that in his mind he left the pasture.

On account of his long delay he started in a flying-run down the lane westward, and had soon passed the hollow and mounted the next rise. He had not yet overtaken his brothers, but he paused to get breath, and looked back. He could see the white figures of the girls in the green enclosure whirling about as they had whirled when he was among them. They seemed to have quite forgotten him already.

All of them, except, perhaps, one. This white shape stood apart by the hedge alone. From her position he knew it to be the pretty maiden with whom he had not danced. Trifling as the matter was, he yet instinctively felt that she was hurt by his oversight. He wished that he had asked her; he wished that he had inquired her name. She was so modest, so expressive, she had looked so soft in her thin white gown that he felt he had acted stupidly.

However, it could not be helped, and turning, and bending himself to a rapid walk, he dismissed the subject from his mind.

Hester Prynne

IN *THE SCARLET LETTER* BY NATHANIEL HAWTHORNE
FIRST PUBLISHED IN: 1850

Who is she? A woman who is made stronger and more virtuous by public scandal.

Her Story

Hester Prynne committed adultery. Her little girl, Pearl, is living proof of her sin, but Hester refuses to tell anyone who fathered her child. The "A" she is forced to wear so prominently on her chest as a public symbol of her adultery is supposed to shame her, but she embroiders the letter with an artistic flair and carries herself about town with such a quiet dignity that people can't help but like her. Over time, people even begin to admire her humble manner and shy smile, which is, of course, an act. Hester is smart enough to know that her life will go more smoothly if she pretends in this way, but in her heart she is not ashamed—she made love to a man she loves dearly and she sees nothing wrong with that.

The man she loves is Reverend Arthur Dimmesdale, and he, whose plan it was to love only God, is in love with Hester. Over the next seven years, their secret affects both of them deeply. For Arthur, the stress and anxiety begin to take a toll on his health. For Hester, quite the opposite happens. She is strengthened by her situation and makes every effort to hold her head up high until it begins to feel like the natural thing to do. Still, Hester is a lonely woman in love and she worries about Arthur Dimmesdale and the burden he feels. If only they could sail away and be a family together in a far away land. If only . . . .

What Makes Hester Prynne So Memorable?

Hester has proven to be among the most quietly courageous and stubbornly loyal women in fiction. She demonstrates dignity and courage at a time when others would lower their heads in shame. She does not show fear, only carefully displayed remorse and a staunch loyalty to her daughter's father. She doesn't genuinely care about the things people think or say. But she is a good mother who knows that her daughter's life will be better if she acts as though she does care—at least a little.

The Life and Times of Nathaniel Hawthorne

Nathaniel Hawthorne, born and reared in Salem, Massachusetts, wanted to be a writer from a very early age. From 1825 to 1836 he wrote short stories and for periodicals. In 1842, he struck up a friendship with Ralph Emerson and Henry David Thoreau, but with a wife (he married Sophia Peabody that same year) and a family to support, he had little time for friendships or anything else that didn't supply a paycheck. The financial burden forced him to accept a position at the Custom House as a surveyor for the Port of Salem. He didn't like the work and for three long years passed the time writing whenever possible.

In 1850, Hawthorne published *The Scarlet Letter*, which finally put his financial problems behind him. In addition to writing more novels, he wrote a campaign biography for President Franklin Pierce, which led to Hawthorne's appointment as consul in England. He and his family moved to England, then to Italy before returning to Massachusetts in 1860. Soon after returning to Massachusetts, Hawthorne began losing weight and feeling ill. Hawthorne died in his sleep at the age of 59 and is buried at Sleepy Hollow in Concord, Massachusetts. Since there was no attending physician when he died no cause of death was recorded.

FROM *The Scarlet Letter*

The door of the jail being flung open from within there appeared, in the first place, like a black shadow emerging into sunshine, the grim and gristly presence of the town-beadle, with a sword by his side, and his staff of office in his hand. This personage prefigured and represented in his aspect the whole dismal severity of the Puritanic code of law, which it was his business to administer in its final and closest application to the offender. Stretching forth the official staff in his left hand, he laid his right upon the shoulder of a young woman, whom he thus drew forward, until, on the threshold of the prison-door, she repelled him, by an action marked with natural dignity and force of character, and stepped into the open air as if by her own free will. She bore in her arms a child, a baby of some three months old, who winked and turned aside its little face from the too vivid light of day; because its existence, heretofore, had brought it acquaintance only with the grey twilight of a dungeon, or other darksome apartment of the prison.

Novel Knowledge: THE SALEM WITCH TRIALS

So ashamed of his great-great-grandfather's role as a judge during the infamous witch trials of Salem, Nathaniel changed his last name from "Hathorne" to the name we know as "Hawthorne" while still a young man.

When the young woman—the mother of this child—stood fully revealed before the crowd, it seemed to be her first impulse to clasp the infant closely to her bosom; not so much by an impulse of motherly affection, as that she might thereby conceal a certain token, which was wrought or fastened into her dress. In a moment, however, wisely judging that one token of her shame would but poorly serve to hide another, she took the baby on her arm, and with a burning blush, and yet a haughty smile, and a glance that would not be abashed, looked around at her townspeople and neighbours. On the breast of her gown, in fine red cloth, surrounded with an elaborate embroidery and fantastic flourishes of gold thread, appeared the letter A. It was so artistically done, and with so much fertility and gorgeous luxuriance of fancy, that it had all the effect of a last and fitting decoration to the apparel which she wore, and which was of a splendour in accordance with the taste of the age, but greatly beyond what was allowed by the sumptuary regulations of the colony.

Novel Knowledge: WHEN YOU HAVE NOTHING GOOD TO SAY

Natives of Salem, Massachusetts, were infuriated by Hawthorne's depiction of them in the book's introduction titled "Custom House." In a reprint of the novel, Hawthorne had the chance to revise the introduction and portray his fellow townspeople in a better light, but he decided he liked it just the way it was.

The young woman was tall, with a figure of perfect elegance on a large scale. She had dark and abundant hair, so glossy that it threw off the sunshine with a gleam; and a face which, besides being beautiful from regularity of feature and richness of complexion, had the impressiveness belonging to a marked brow and deep black eyes. She was ladylike, too, after the manner of the feminine gentility of those days; characterised by a certain state and dignity, rather than by the delicate, evanescent, and indescribable grace which is now recognised as its indication.

And never had Hester Prynne appeared more ladylike, in the antique interpretation of the term, than as she issued from the prison. Those who had before known her, and had expected to behold her dimmed and obscured by a disastrous cloud, were astonished, and even startled, to perceive how her beauty shone out, and made a halo of the misfortune and ignominy in which she was enveloped. It may be true that, to a sensitive observer, there was some thing exquisitely painful in it. Her attire, which indeed, she had wrought for the occasion in prison, and had modelled much after her own fancy, seemed to express the attitude of her spirit, the desperate recklessness of her mood, by its wild and picturesque peculiarity. But the point which drew all eyes, and, as it were, transfigured the wearer—so that both men and women who had been familiarly acquainted with Hester Prynne were now impressed as if they beheld her for the first time—was that SCARLET LETTER, so fantastically embroidered and illuminated upon her bosom. It had the effect of a spell, taking her out of the ordinary relations with humanity, and enclosing her in a sphere by herself.

"She hath good skill at her needle, that's certain," remarked one of her female spectators; "but did ever a woman, before this brazen hussy, contrive such a way of showing it? Why, gossips, what is it but to laugh in the faces of our godly magistrates, and make a pride out of what they, worthy gentlemen, meant for a punishment?"

"It were well," muttered the most iron-visaged of the old dames, "if we stripped Madame Hester's rich gown off her dainty shoulders; and as for the red letter which she hath stitched so curiously,

I'll bestow a rag of mine own rheumatic flannel to make a fitter one!"

"Oh, peace, neighbours—peace!" whispered their youngest companion; "do not let her hear you! Not a stitch in that embroidered letter but she has felt it in her heart."

The grim beadle now made a gesture with his staff. "Make way, good people—make way, in the King's name!" cried he. "Open a passage; and I promise ye, Mistress Prynne shall be set where man, woman, and child may have a fair sight of her brave apparel from this time till an hour past meridian. A blessing on the righteous colony of the Massachusetts, where iniquity is dragged out into the sunshine! Come along, Madame Hester, and show your scarlet letter in the market-place!"

A lane was forthwith opened through the crowd of spectators. Preceded by the beadle, and attended by an irregular procession of stern-browed men and unkindly visaged women, Hester Prynne set forth towards the place appointed for her punishment. A crowd of eager and curious schoolboys, understanding little of the matter in hand, except that it gave them a half-holiday, ran before her progress, turning their heads continually to stare into her face and at the winking baby in her arms, and at the ignominious letter on her breast. It was no great distance, in those days, from the prison door to the market-place. Measured by the prisoner's experience, however, it might be reckoned a journey of some length; for haughty as her demeanour was, she perchance underwent an agony from every footstep of those that thronged to see her, as if her heart had been flung into the street for them all to spurn and trample upon. In our nature, however, there is a provision, alike marvellous and merciful, that the sufferer should never know the intensity of what he endures by its present torture, but chiefly by the pang that rankles after it. With almost a serene deportment, therefore, Hester Prynne passed through this portion of her ordeal, and came to a sort of scaffold, at the western extremity of the market-place. It stood nearly beneath the eaves of Boston's earliest church, and appeared to be a fixture there.

In fact, this scaffold constituted a portion of a penal machine, which now, for two or three generations past, has been merely historical and traditionary among us, but was held, in the old time, to be as effectual an agent, in the promotion of good citizenship, as ever was the guillotine among the terrorists of France. It was, in short, the platform of the pillory; and above it rose the framework of that instrument of discipline, so fashioned as to confine the human head in its tight grasp, and thus hold it up to the public gaze. The very ideal of ignominy was embodied and made manifest in this contrivance of wood and iron. There can be no outrage, methinks, against our common nature—whatever be the delinquencies of the individual—no outrage more flagrant than to forbid the culprit to hide his face for shame; as it was the essence of this punishment to do. In Hester Prynne's instance, however, as not unfrequently in other cases, her sentence bore that she should stand a certain time upon the platform, but without undergoing that gripe about the neck and confinement of the head, the proneness to which was the most devilish characteristic of this ugly engine. Knowing well her part, she ascended a flight of wooden steps, and was thus displayed to the surrounding multitude, at about the height of a man's shoulders above the street.

Had there been a Papist among the crowd of Puritans, he might have seen in this beautiful woman, so picturesque in her attire and mien, and with the infant at her bosom, an object to remind him of the image of Divine Maternity, which so many illustrious painters have vied with one another to represent; something which should remind him, indeed, but only by contrast, of that sacred image of sinless motherhood, whose infant was to redeem the world. Here, there was the taint of deepest sin in the most sacred quality of human life, working such effect, that the world was only the darker for this woman's beauty, and the more lost for the infant that she had borne.

The scene was not without a mixture of awe, such as must always invest the spectacle of guilt and shame in a fellow-creature, before society shall have grown corrupt enough to smile, instead of shuddering at it. The witnesses of Hester Prynne's disgrace had not yet passed beyond their simplicity. They were stern enough to look upon her death, had that been the sentence, without a murmur at its severity, but had none of the heartlessness of another social state, which would find only a theme for jest in an exhibition like the present. Even had there been a disposition to turn the matter into ridicule, it must have been repressed and overpowered by the solemn presence of men no less dignified than the governor, and several of his counsellors, a judge, a general, and the ministers of the town, all of whom sat or stood in a balcony of the meeting-house, looking down upon the platform. When such personages could constitute a part of the spectacle, without risking the majesty, or reverence of rank and office, it was safely to be inferred that the infliction of a legal sentence would have an earnest and effectual meaning. Accordingly, the crowd was sombre and grave. The unhappy culprit sustained herself as best a woman might, under the heavy weight of a thousand unrelenting eyes, all fastened upon her, and concentrated at her bosom. It was almost intolerable to be borne. Of an impulsive and passionate nature, she had fortified herself to encounter the stings and venomous stabs of public contumely, wreaking itself in every variety of insult; but there was a quality so much more terrible in the solemn mood of the popular mind, that she longed rather to behold all those rigid countenances contorted with scornful merriment, and herself the object. Had a roar of laughter burst from the multitude—each man, each woman, each little shrill-voiced child, contributing their individual parts—Hester Prynne might have repaid them all with a bitter and disdainful smile. But, under the leaden infliction which it was her doom to endure, she felt, at moments, as if she must needs shriek out with the full power of her lungs, and cast herself from the scaffold down upon the ground, or else go mad at once.

Yet there were intervals when the whole scene, in which she was the most conspicuous object, seemed to vanish from her eyes, or, at least, glimmered indistinctly before them, like a mass of imperfectly shaped and spectral images. Her mind, and especially her memory, was preternaturally active, and kept bringing up other scenes than this roughly hewn street of a little town, on the edge of the western wilderness: other faces than were lowering upon her from beneath the brims of those steeple-crowned hats. Reminiscences, the most trifling and immaterial, passages of infancy and school-days, sports, childish quarrels, and the little domestic traits of her maiden years, came swarming back upon her, intermingled with recollections of whatever was gravest in her subsequent life; one picture precisely as vivid as another; as if all were of similar importance, or all alike a play. Possibly, it was an instinctive device of her spirit to relieve itself by the exhibition of these phantasmagoric forms, from the cruel weight and hardness of the reality.

Be that as it might, the scaffold of the pillory was a point of view that revealed to Hester Prynne the entire track along which she had been treading, since her happy infancy. Standing on that miserable eminence, she saw again her native village, in Old England, and her paternal home: a decayed house of grey stone, with a poverty-stricken aspect, but retaining a half obliterated shield of arms over the portal, in token of antique gentility. She saw her father's face, with its bold brow, and reverend white beard that flowed over the old-fashioned Elizabethan ruff; her mother's, too, with the look of heedful and anxious love which it always wore in her remembrance, and which, even since her death, had so often laid the impediment of a gentle remonstrance in her daughter's pathway. She saw her own face, glowing with girlish beauty, and illuminating all the interior of the dusky mirror in which she had been wont to gaze at it. There she beheld another countenance, of a man well stricken in years, a pale, thin, scholar-like visage, with eyes dim and bleared by the lamp-light that had served them to pore over many ponderous books. Yet those same bleared optics had a strange, penetrating power, when it was their owner's purpose to read the human soul. This figure of the study and the cloister, as Hester Prynne's womanly fancy failed not to recall, was slightly deformed, with the left shoulder a trifle higher than the right. Next rose before her in memory's picture-gallery, the intricate and narrow thoroughfares, the tall, grey houses, the huge cathedrals, and the public edifices, ancient in date and quaint in architecture, of a continental city; where new life had awaited her, still in connexion with the misshapen scholar: a new life, but feeding itself on time-worn materials, like a tuft of green moss on a crumbling wall. Lastly, in lieu of these shifting scenes, came back the rude market-place of the Puritan settlement, with all the townspeople assembled, and levelling their stern regards at Hester Prynne—yes, at herself—who stood on the scaffold of the pillory, an infant on her arm, and the letter A, in scarlet, fantastically embroidered with gold thread, upon her bosom.

Could it be true? She clutched the child so fiercely to her breast that it sent forth a cry; she turned her eyes downward at the scarlet letter, and even touched it with her finger, to assure herself that the infant and the shame were real. Yes these were her realities—all else had vanished!

Maria Chapdelaine

IN *MARIA CHAPDELAINE* BY LOUIS HÉMON

FIRST PUBLISHED IN: 1914 (TRANSLATED BY W. H. BLAKE IN 1921)

> *Who is she?* A resilient, mature teenager torn between her desire to see the world and her sense of duty to her family.

Her Story

At age fifteen, Maria Chapdelaine has her life planned. She will marry François Paradis and live in the Canadian wild—the only land she has ever known. But when François dies in a terrible blizzard, Maria's plans die with him. She begins to question everything about her future, and becomes more confused when two young men vie for her affection. First, Maria's childhood friend, Lorenzo, visits from Boston and proposes marriage. He captivates her with stories of life in the city. Then Eutrope decides he should make his feelings known too. He has loved Maria for years, but always knew that he couldn't compete with François. Neither one stirs feelings in her the way François did, but listening to Eutrope talk about his dream of building a home with her, and living on a farm (that is, more of the same), Maria begins to think of Lorenzo's proposal as a wonderful adventure. Maria is ready to tell Lorenzo yes, when her mother suddenly falls ill and dies. With her Mother gone, Maria's sense of duty to her family and her sense of adventure are at odds. Her father seems helpless, and her little sister, Alma Rose, has no mother. Maria knows her mother would have wanted her to follow her heart. But wouldn't she also want her to raise Alma Rose? Would she expect Maria to be true to her family or true to herself? Her future, once so simple and well-defined, grows more complicated and confusing than she could ever have imagined.

What Makes Maria Chapdelaine So Memorable?

Living in the wilderness so close to nature—so close to life as well as death—creates a pragmatic quality in Maria that is rare for a teenager. Growing up in such harsh conditions seems to prepare her for the hardships that life has in store for her. She remains calm and thoughtful as she stumbles into womanhood facing heartache, tough choices, and the instant responsibilities her mother left behind when she passed. Still, it is easy to imagine Maria lying in bed at night and wondering, what if? What if?

The Life and Times of Louis Hémon

Louis Hémon was born in France in 1880 and lived with his family in Paris. He studied law and languages at the Sorbonne before moving to London to be a sports writer. While in England he met a young woman named Lydia O'Kelly, and they had a daughter together. However, even fatherhood could not keep this wanderer in one place for long. In 1911, Hémon moved to Canada, and lived briefly in Montreal before going to work on a farm in Lac Saint-Jean, which is where he wrote *Maria Chapdelaine*. Unfortunately, Hémon didn't live to see his novel published—in July of 1913, he was struck and killed by a train.

FROM *Maria Chapdelaine*

One evening in February Samuel Chapdelaine said to his daughter: "The roads are passable; if you wish it, Maria, we shall go to La Pipe on Sunday for the mass."

"Very well, father;" but she replied in a voice so dejected, almost indifferent, that her parents exchanged glances behind her back.

Country folk do not die for love, nor spend the rest of their days nursing a wound. They are too near to nature, and know too well the stern laws that rule their lives. Thus it is perhaps, that they are sparing of high-sounding words; choosing to say "liking" rather than "loving" . . . "ennui" rather than "grief," that so the joys and sorrows of the heart may bear a fit proportion to those more anxious concerns of life which have to do with their daily toil, the yield of their lands, provision for the future.

Maria did not for a moment dream that life for her was over, or that the world must henceforward be a sad wilderness, because Francis Paradis would not return in the spring nor ever again. But her heart was aching, and while sorrow possessed it the future held no promise for her.

When Sunday arrived, father and daughter early began to make ready for the two hours' journey which would bring them to St. Henri de Taillon, and the church. Before half-past seven Charles Eugene was harnessed, and Maria, still wearing a heavy winter cloak, had carefully deposited in her purse the list of her mother's commissions. A few minutes later the sleigh-bells were tinkling, and the rest of the family grouped themselves at the little square window to watch the departure.

For the first hour the horse could not go beyond a walk, sinking knee-deep in snow; for only the Chapdelaines used this road, laid out and cleared by themselves, and not enough travelled to become smooth and hard. But when they reached the beaten highway Charles Eugene trotted along briskly.

They passed through Honfleur, a hamlet of eight scattered houses, and then re-entered the woods. After a time they came upon clearings, then houses appeared dotted along the road; little by little the dusky ranks of the forest retreated, and soon they were in the village with other sleighs before and following them, all going toward the church.

Novel Knowledge: A FRENCH-CANADIAN CLASSIC

Initially serialized in 1914 in a Paris magazine, *Le Temps, Maria Chapdelaine* was put into book form in 1916. The story, well-received during its time, is now considered a French-Canadian classic. The novel has been translated into more than twenty languages in twenty-three countries. It was made into a movie in 1950 and again in 1983.

Since the beginning of the year Maria had gone three times to hear mass at St. Henri de Taillon, which the people of the country persist in calling La Pipe, as in the gallant days of the first settlers. For her, besides being an exercise of piety, this was almost the only distraction possible and her father sought to furnish it whenever he could do so, believing that the impressive rites of the church and a meeting with acquaintances in the village would help to banish her grief.

On this occasion when the mass was ended, instead of paying visits they went to the curees house. It was already thronged with members of the congregation from remote farms, for the Canadian priest not only has the consciences of his flock in charge, but is their counsellor in all affairs, and the composer of their disputes; the solitary individual of different station to whom they can resort for the solving of their difficulties.

The cure of St. Henri sent none away empty who asked his advice; some he dealt with in a few swift words amidst a general conversation where he bore his cheerful part; others at greater length in the privacy of an adjoining room. When the turn of the Chapdelaines came he looked at his watch.

"We shall have dinner first. What say you, my good friends? You must have found an appetite on the road. As for myself, singing mass makes me hungry beyond anything you could believe."

He laughed heartily, more tickled than anyone at his own joke, and led his guests into the dining-room. Another priest was there from a neighbouring parish, and two or three farmers. The meal was one long discussion about husbandry, with a few amusing stories and bits of harmless gossip thrown in; now and then one of the farmers, suddenly remembering where he was, would labour some pious remark which the priests acknowledged with a nod or an absent-minded "Yes! Yes!"

Novel Knowledge: BIOGRAPHIES

Despite publishing only one novel, there are two biographical works about Louis Hémon. *L'aventure Louis Hémon* (1974) by Alfred Ayotte and Victor Tremblay, and *Louis Hémon, le fou du lac* (2000) by Mathieu-Robert Sauvé.

The dinner over at last, some of the guests departed after lighting their pipes. The cure, catching a glance from Chapdelaine, seemed to recall something; arising, he motioned to Maria, and went before her into the next room which served him both for visitors and as his office.

A small harmonium stood against the wall; on the other side was a table with agricultural journals, a Civil Code and a few books bound in black leather; on the walls hung a portrait of Pius X., an engraving of the Holy Family, the coloured broadside of a Quebec merchant with sleighs and threshing-machines side by side, and a number of official notices as to precautions against forest fires and epidemics amongst cattle.

Turning to Maria, the cure said kindly enough;—"So it appears that you are distressing yourself beyond what is reasonable and right?"

She looked at him humbly, not far from believing that the priest's supernatural power had divined her trouble without need of telling. He inclined his tall figure, and bent toward her his thin peasant face; for beneath the robe was still the tiller of the soil: the gaunt and yellow visage, the cautious eyes, the huge bony shoulders. Even his hands—hands wont to dispense the favours of Heaven—were those of the husbandman, with swollen veins beneath the dark skin. But Maria saw in him only the priest, the cure of the parish, appointed of God to interpret life to her and show her the path of duty.

"Be seated there," he said, pointing to a chair. She sat down somewhat like a schoolgirl who is to have a scolding, somewhat like a woman in a sorcerer's den who awaits in mingled hope and dread the working of his unearthly spells ... ...

An hour later the sleigh was speeding over the hard snow. Chapdelaine drowsed, and the reins were slipping from his open hands. Rousing himself and lifting his head, he sang again in full-voiced fervour the hymn he was singing as they left the village:—

. . . Adorons-le dans le ciel.

Adorons-le sur l'autel . . .

Then he fell silent, his chin dropping slowly toward his breast, and the only sound upon the road was the tinkle of sleigh-bells.

Maria was thinking of the priest's words: "If there was affection between you it is very proper that you should know regret. But you were not pledged to one another, because neither you nor he had spoken to your parents; therefore it is not befitting or right that you should sorrow thus, nor feel so deep a grief for a young man who, after all is said, was nothing to you . . ."

And again: "That masses should be sung, that you should pray for him, such things are useful and good, you could do no better. Three high masses with music, and three more when the boys return from the woods, as your father has asked me, most assuredly these will help him, and also you may be certain they will delight him more than your lamentations, since they will shorten by so much his time of expiation. But to grieve like this, and to go about casting gloom over the household is not well, nor is it pleasing in the sight of God."

He did not appear in the guise of a comforter, nor of one who gives counsel in the secret affairs of the heart, but rather as a man of the law or a chemist who enunciates his bald formulas, invariable and unfailing.

"The duty of a girl like you—good-looking, healthy, active withal and a clever housewife—is in the first place to help her old parents, and in good time to marry and bring up a Christian family of her own. You have no call to the religious life? No. Then you must give up torturing yourself in this fashion, because it is a sacrilegious thing and unseemly, seeing that the young man was nothing whatever to you. The good God knows what is best for us; we should neither rebel nor complain . . ."

In all this, but one phrase left Maria a little doubting, it was the priest's assurance that Francois Paradis, in the place where now he was, cared only for masses to repose his soul, and never at all for the deep and tender regrets lingering behind him. This she could not constrain herself to believe. Unable to think of him otherwise in death than in life, she felt it must bring him something of happiness and consolation that her sorrow was keeping alive their ineffectual love for a little space beyond death. Yet, since the priest had said it . . .

The road wound its way among the trees rising sombrely from the snow. Here and there a squirrel, alarmed by the swiftly passing sleigh and the tinkling bells, sprang upon a trunk and scrambled upward, clinging to the bark. From the gray sky a biting cold was falling and the wind stung the cheek, for this was February, with two long months of winter yet to come.

As Charles Eugene trotted along the beaten road, bearing the travellers to their lonely house, Maria, in obedience to the words of the cure at St. Henri, strove to drive away gloom and put mourning from her; as simple-mindedly as she would have fought the temptation of a dance, of a doubtful amusement or anything that was plainly wrong and hence forbidden.

They reached home as night was falling. The coming of evening was only a slow fading of the light, for, since morning, the heavens had been overcast, the sun obscured. A sadness rested upon the pallid earth; the firs and cypresses did not wear the aspect of living trees and the naked birches seemed to doubt of the springtime. Maria shivered as she left the sleigh, and hardly noticed Chien, barking and gambolling a welcome, or the children who called to her from the door-step. The world seemed strangely empty, for this evening at least. Love was snatched away, and they forbade remembrance. She went swiftly into the house without looking about her, conscious of a new dread and hatred for the bleak land, the forest's eternal shade, the snow and the cold,—for all those things she had lived her life amongst, which now had wounded her.

Janie Crawford

IN *THEIR EYES WERE WATCHING GOD*
BY ZORA NEALE HURSTON
FIRST PUBLISHED IN: 1937

Who is she? An independent woman who realizes that while she wants love, she needs respect more.

Her Story

Janie Crawford is a beautiful black woman who wants love and respect from her husband. It never occurs to her that she might be asking for too much.

Janie first marries Logan Killicks, a poor-excuse for a man who wants a farm hand more than a wife; then Jody Starks, a slick, ambitious man who treats her like a prize show horse. By the time twenty years of marriage has played out and Jody dies, Janie is so glad to see him gone that she doesn't even pretend to grieve. Instead, she revels in her freedom.

When Janie is almost forty years old, a twenty-five-year-old man who people call Tea Cake comes along. Janie is suspicious of any man who shows an interest in her, especially a man practically half her age, but Tea Cake swears it's love at first sight and tells Janie that he likes the challenge. Eventually swayed, Janie moves to the Everglades with him. For the first time in her life she is happy. Unfortunately, Janie's happiness is cut short. When a hurricane hits she and Tea Cake are chased out of their home by floodwaters and are then bitten by a rabid dog. They must fight just to stay alive. Together, they endure more pain—and experience more love—than Janie ever thought possible.

What Makes Janie Crawford So Memorable?

Janie—like so many other women—wants a man who will love her. But she also wants, and eventually demands, a man who will respect her. Faced with a hard, bleak life as a black woman in the 1920s, she is strong, independent, and proud. She isn't an ambitious woman. There is no particular cause she wants to fight. At times she may seem lazy, even a bit ungrateful for what she has, but Janie has always known what she wants and is unwilling to settle for the first (or second) thing that comes along.

The Life and Times of Zora Neale Hurston

Born in Notasulga, Alabama, in 1891, Zora Neale Hurston grew up in Eatonville, Florida. After graduating with her associate's degree from Howard University, she moved to New York and became a part of the Harlem Renaissance, a group of black artists. Hurston married twice, but both relationships ended in divorce.

With one novel to her credit, she went to Haiti in March of 1937, where she wrote *Their Eyes Were Watching God*. The novel was published in September of the same year. Two years later, she joined the faculty of North Carolina College for Negroes in Durham, but while there she was accused of sexually assaulting a young boy. Though she proved her innocence, the scandal destroyed her reputation. Eventually, Hurston returned to Florida, where she freelanced for magazines, worked at a library, and took a job as a motel housekeeper. In 1960, she died penniless at the St. Lucie County Welfare Home in Fort Pierce, Florida.

FROM *Their Eyes Were Watching God*

Janie wanted to ask Hezekiah about Tea Cake, but she was afraid he might misunderstand her and think she was interested. In the first place he looked too young for her. Must be around twenty-five and here *she* was around forty. Then again he didn't look like he had too much. Maybe he was hanging around to get in with her and strip her of all that she had. Just as well if she never saw him again. He was probably the kind of man who lived with various women but never married. Fact is, she decided to treat him so cold if he ever did foot the place that he'd be sure not to come hanging around there again.

Novel Knowledge: THE REAL PLACE

Just as Hurston describes in *Their Eyes Were Watching God*, the town of Eatonville was truly the first all–African American town to be incorporated after the Emancipation Proclamation in 1863. The town is six miles north of Orlando. Every year Eatonville celebrates Hurston's life and works with the Zora Fest.

He waited a week exactly to come back for Janie's snub. It was early in the afternoon and she and Hezekiah were alone. She heard somebody humming like they were feeling for pitch and looked towards the door. Tea Cake stood there mimicking the tuning of a guitar. He frowned and struggled with the pegs of his imaginary instrument watching her out of the corner of his eye with that secret joke playing over his face. Finally she smiled and he sung middle C, put his guitar under his arm and walked on back to where she was.

"Evenin', folks. Thought y'all might lak uh lil music this evenin' so Ah brought long mah box."

"Crazy thing!" Janie commented, beaming out with light.

He acknowledged the compliment with a smile and sat down on a box. "Anybody have uh Coca-Cola wid me?"

"Ah just had one," Janie temporized with her conscience.

"It'll hafter be done all over agin, Mis' Starks."

"How come?"

"'Cause it wasn't done right dat time. 'Kiah bring us two bottles from de bottom ud de box."

"How you been makin' out since Ah see yuh last, Tea Cake?"

"Can't kick. Could be worse. Made four days dis week and got de pay in mah pocket."

"We got a rich man round here, then. Buyin' passenger trains uh battleships this week?"

"Which one do *you* want?" It all depends on you."

"Oh, if you'se treatin' me tuh it, Ah b'lieve Ah'll take de passenger train. If it blow up Ah'll still be on land."

"Choose de battleship if dat's whut you really want. Ah know where one is right now. Seen one round Key West de other day."

"How you gointuh git it?"

"Ah shucks, dem Admirals is always ole folks. Can't no ole man stop me from gittin' no ship for yuh if dat's whut you want. Ah'd git dat ship out from under him so slick till he'd be walkin' de water lak ole Peter befo' he knowed it."

They played away the evening again. Everybody was surprised at Janie playing checkers but they liked it. Three or four stood behind her and coached her moves and generally made merry with her in a restrained way. Finally everybody went home but Tea Cake.

"You kin close up, 'Kiah," Janie said. "Think Ah'll g'wan home."

Tea Cake fell in beside her and mounted the porch this time. So she offered him a seat and they made a lot of laughter out of nothing. Near eleven o'clock she remembered a piece of pound cake she had put away. Tea Cake went out to the lemon tree at the corner of the kitchen and picked some lemons and squeezed them for her. So they had lemonade too.

"Moon's too pretty fuh anybody tuh be sleepin' it away," Tea Cake said after they had washed up the plates and glasses. "Less us go fishin'."

"Fishin'? Dis time uh night?"

"Unhhunh, fishin'. Ah know where de bream is beddin'. Seen 'em when Ah come round de lake dis evenin'. Where's yo' fishin' poles? Less go set on de lake."

It was so crazy digging worms by lamp light and setting out for Lake Sabelia after midnight that she felt like a child breaking rules. That's what made Janie like it. They caught two or three and got home just before day. Then she had to smuggle Tea Cake out by the back gate and that made it seem like some great secret she was keeping from the town.

"Mis' Janie," Hezekiah began sullenly next day, "you oughtn't 'low dat Tea Cake tuh be walkin' tuh de house wid yuh. Ah'll go wid yuh mahself after dis, if you'se skeered."

"What's de matter wid Tea Cake, 'Kiah? Is he uh thief uh somethin'?"

"Ah ain't never heard nobody say he stole nothin'."

"Is he bad 'bout totin' pistols and knives tuh hurt people wid?"

"Dey don't say he ever cut nobody or shot nobody neither."

"Well, is he—he—is he got uh wife or something lak dat? Not dat it's any uh mah business." She held her breath for the answer.

Novel Knowledge: THE STORM OF THE CENTURY

The hurricane Hurston writes about with such force in the novel is the Okeechobee Hurricane, or Hurricane San Felipe Segundo—a devastating hurricane that hit Florida in September 1928.

"No'm. And nobody wouldn't marry Tea Cake tuh starve tuh death lessen it's somebody jes lak him—ain't used to nothin'. 'Course he always keep hisself in changin' clothes. Dat long-legged Tea Cake ain't got doodly squat. He ain't got no business makin' hisself familiar wid nobody lak you. Ah said Ah wuz goin' to tell yuh so yuh could know."

"Oh dat's all right, Hezekiah. Thank yuh mighty much."

The next night when she mounted her steps Tea Cake was there before her, sitting on the porch in the dark. He had a string of fresh-caught trout for a present.

"Ah'll clean 'em, you fry 'em and let's eat," he said with the assurance of not being refused. They went out into the kitchen and fixed up the hot fish and corn muffins and ate. Then Tea Cake went to the piano without so much as asking and began playing blues and singing, and throwing grins over his shoulder. The sounds lulled Janie to soft slumber and she woke up with Tea Cake combing her hair and scratching the dandruff from her scalp. It made her more comfortable and drowsy.

"Tea Cake, where you git uh comb from tuh be combin' mah hair wid?"

"Ah brought it wid me. Come prepared tuh lay mah hands on it tuhnight."

"Why, Tea Cake? Whut good do combin' mah hair do *you?* It's *mah* comfortable, not yourn."

"It's mine too. Ah ain't been sleepin' so good for more'n uh week cause Ah been wishin' so bad tuh git mah hands in yo' hair. It's so pretty. It feels jus' lak underneath uh dove's wing next to mah face."

"Umph! You'se mighty easy satisfied. Ah been had dis same hair next tuh mah face ever since Ah cried de fust time, and 'tain't never gimme me no thrill."

"Ah tell you lak you told me—you'se mighty hard tuh satisfy. Ah betcha dem lips don't satisfy yuh neither."

"Dat's right, Tea Cake. They's dere and Ah make use of 'em whenever it's necessary, but nothin' special tuh me."

"Umph! umph! umph! Ah betcha you don't never go tuh de lookin' glass and enjoy yo' eyes yo'self. You lets other folks git all de enjoyment out of 'em 'thout takin' in any of it yo'self."

"Naw, Ah never gazes at 'em in de lookin' glass. If anybody else gits any pleasure out of 'em Ah ain't been told about it."

"See dat? You'se got de world in uh jug and make out you don't know it. But Ah'm glad tuh be de one tuh tell yuh."

"Ah guess you done told plenty women all about it."

"Ah'm de Apostle Paul tuh de Gentiles. Ah tells 'em and then agin Ah shows 'em."

"Ah thought so." She yawned and made to get up from the sofa. "You done got me so sleepy wid yo' head-scratchin' Ah kin hardly make it tuh de bed." She stood up at once, collecting her hair. He sat still.

"Naw, you ain't sleepy, Mis' Janie. You jus' want me tuh go. You figger Ah'm uh rounder and uh pimp and you done wasted too much time talkin' wid me."

"Why, Tea Cake! Whut ever put dat notion in yo' head?"

"De way you looked at me when Ah said whut Ah did. Yo' face skeered me so bad till mah whiskers drawed up."

"Ah ain't got no business bein' mad at nothin' you do and say. You got it all wrong. Ah ain't mad atall."

"Ah know it and dat's what puts de shamery on me. You'se jus' disgusted wid me. Yo' face jus' left here and went off somewhere else.

Naw, you ain't mad wid me. Ah be glad if you was, 'cause then Ah might do somethin' tuh please yuh. But lak it is—"

"Mah likes and dislikes ought not tuh make no difference wid you, Tea Cake. Dat's fuh yo' lady friend. Ah'm jus' uh sometime friend uh yourn."

Janie walked towards the stairway slowly, and Tea Cake sat where he was, as if he had frozen to his seat, in fear that once he got up, he'd never get back in it again. He swallowed hard and looked at her walk away.

"Ah didn't aim tuh let on tuh yuh 'bout it, leastways not right away, but Ah ruther be shot wid tacks than fuh you tuh act wid me lak you is right now. You got me in de go-long."

At the newel post Janie whirled around and for the space of a thought she was lit up like a transfiguration. Her next thought brought her crashing down. *He's just saying anything for the time being, feeling he's got me so I'll b'lieve him.* The next thought buried her under tons of cold futility. *He's trading on being younger than me. Getting ready to laugh at me for an old fool. But oh, what wouldn't I give to be twelve years younger so I could b'lieve him!*

"Aw, Tea Cake, you just say dat tuhnight because de fish and corn bread tasted sort of good. Tomorrow yo' mind would change."

"Naw, it wouldn't neither. Ah know better."

"Anyhow from what you told me when we wuz back dere in de kitchen Ah'm nearly twelve years older than you."

"Ah done thought all about dat and tried tuh struggle aginst it, but it don't do me no good. De thought uh mah youngness don't satisfy me lak yo' presence do."

"It makes uh whole heap uh difference wid most folks, Tea Cake."

"Things lak dat got uh whole lot tuh do wid convenience, but it ain't got nothin' tuh do wid love."

"Well, Ah love tuh find out whut you think after sun-up tomorrow. Dis is jus' yo' night thought."

"You got yo' ideas and Ah got mine. Ah got uh dollar dat says you'se wrong. But Ah reckon you don't bet money, neither."

"Ah never have done it so fur. But as de old folks always say, Ah'm born but Ah ain't dead. No tellin' whut Ah'm liable tuh do yet."

He got up suddenly and took his hat. "Good night, Mis' Janie. Look lak we done run our conversation from grass roots tuh pine trees. G'bye." He almost ran out of the door.

Isabel Archer

IN *PORTRAIT OF A LADY* BY HENRY JAMES

FIRST PUBLISHED IN: 1880–1881

Who is she? A free-spirited woman is brought to her knees by the scandalous greed of others.

Her Story

Isabel Archer is a woman with a wild, adventurous spirit who is certain that marriage will ruin any chance she has of living life to the fullest. When her parents die, Isabel goes to live with Mr. Touchett, her wealthy uncle, and Ralph, her cousin and best friend. Ralph loves her independent spirit, and wishes he could live long enough to see what life has in store for her, but he is sick and knows he is not long for this world. After seeing Isabel turn down marriage proposals from both Lord Warburton and Casper Goodwood, a man she genuinely cares for, Ralph knows she is serious about avoiding marriage. He asks his dying father to leave his inheritance to Isabel so she can see the world on her own terms. His father grants his wish and Isabel is soon a rich woman. Ralph is thrilled, but not everyone is as happy with Isabel's fortune.

Madame Merle, a longtime companion to Mr. Touchett, inherits nothing. She befriends Isabel and devises a plan with an old lover, Gilbert Osmond. Osmond, an ego manic who wants money but sees himself as a man above work, seduces Isabel in a way she has never known before. He is far more coy than the other men who wanted Isabel to be their wife. They were, after all, sincere and he is not. Over time,

Osmond convinces Isabel that her freedom will not be in jeopardy if she becomes his wife. Ralph, who sees Osmond for the con man he really is, tries to talk Isabel out of marrying, but she refuses to listen. Soon after they are married, Osmond tortures Isabel with psychological games and absurd accusations and he spends her money on lavish, selfish things. Isabel is miserable. When Ralph visits her in Italy, she is embarrassed and cool toward him. It hurts Ralph to see his cousin so sad. He returns to England knowing he will soon die, and he wonders if he will ever see Isabel again.

When Isabel learns that Ralph only has a few days left to live, she begs Gilbert to let her go to England. He forbids it. But Gilbert's sister decides enough is enough, and she reveals the elaborate plan Gilbert and Madame Merle concocted in order to live off of Isabel's money. With this new revelation, a betrayed and angry Isabel finds the strength to leave Italy and go to England to be with Ralph. Once home, she tends to her cousin's every need, while trying to sort out the mess she has made of her life. After Ralph dies, Isabel resists her friends' help and runs away. Where she goes, or what she does next is anyone's guess.

Novel Knowledge: JAMES'S INFLUENCE ON HEMINGWAY

As a young man, Ernest Hemingway criticized James's work. As Hemingway grew older, it seems his opinions may have changed. In 1954, a depressed Hemingway wrote in a letter to a friend, "Pretty soon I will have to throw this away so I better try to be calm like Henry James. Did you ever read Henry James? He was a great writer who came to Venice and looked out the window and smoked his cigar and thought."

What Makes Isabel Archer So Memorable?

Before Isabel Archer came along few women characters were revealed so profoundly through their most private thoughts and sexual fantasies. The intimacy between Isabel and the reader makes her hard to forget and easy to care for on a deeper level. Even her desires are made known, which feels like a privilege since she takes on a cold, distant manner with the people who were once her friends. When she makes bad decisions—and she makes quite a few—we understand her so well that we are not surprised, only frustrated and supportive.

The Life and Times of Henry James

A native of New York, James was born into a wealthy family that frequently traveled back and forth between Europe and America during his youth. This travel bug took hold and, after leaving Harvard Law School to be a writer, he decided that he preferred living abroad. He began writing his first novel, *Watch and Ward*, while traveling through Venice and moved to Paris in the early 1870s where he began writing for the *New York Tribune*. As much as he liked Paris and admired the Parisian sense of style and taste, James didn't feel at home there, so in 1876 he moved to England where he lived for the rest of his life; he was finally granted citizenship in 1915. One year later, James unfortunately suffered a stroke and died in London. His ashes were sent to Cambridge, Massachusetts.

Though he had many opportunities, James never married; he referred to himself as a confirmed bachelor. Still, women were at the forefront of his mind. His main characters were often young American women in abusive and oppressive situations. The way women were treated in society deeply troubled James. His novels, including *Portrait of a Lady*, often also deal with the cultural and psychological differences between Europeans and Americans. Isabel Archer, wide-eyed and ready to take on the world, represents the American spirit, while the older, more clever characters tend to represent the old world values found in Europe. What happens when these worlds collide intrigued James to no end.

From *Portrait of a Lady*

She had had no hidden motive in wishing him not to take her home; it simply struck her that for some days past she had consumed an inordinate quantity of his time, and the independent spirit of the American girl whom extravagance of aid places in an attitude that she ends by finding "affected" had made her decide that for these few hours she must suffice to herself. She had moreover a great fondness for intervals of solitude, which since her arrival in England had been but meagrely met. It was a luxury she could always command at home and she had wittingly missed it. That evening, however, an incident occurred which—had there been a critic to note it—would have taken all colour from the theory that the wish to be quite by herself had caused her to dispense with her cousin's attendance. Seated toward nine o'clock in the dim illumination of Pratt's Hotel and trying with the aid of two tall candles to lose herself in a volume she had brought from Gardencourt, she succeeded only to the extent of reading other words than those printed on the page—words that Ralph had spoken to her that afternoon. Suddenly the well-muffed knuckle of the waiter was applied to the door, which presently gave way to his exhibition, even as a glorious trophy, of the card of a visitor. When this memento had offered to her fixed sight the name of Mr. Caspar Goodwood she let the man stand before her without signifying her wishes.

"Shall I show the gentleman up, ma'am?" he asked with a slightly encouraging inflexion.

Isabel hesitated still and while she hesitated glanced at the mirror. "He may come in," she said at last; and waited for him not so much smoothing her hair as girding her spirit.

Caspar Goodwood was accordingly the next moment shaking hands with her, but saying nothing till the servant had left the room. "Why didn't you answer my letter?" he then asked in a quick, full, slightly peremptory tone—the tone of a man whose questions were habitually pointed and who was capable of much insistence.

She answered by a ready question, "How did you know I was here?"

"Miss Stackpole let me know," said Caspar Goodwood. "She told me you would probably be at home alone this evening and would be willing to see me."

"Where did she see you—to tell you that?"

"She didn't see me; she wrote to me."

Isabel was silent; neither had sat down; they stood there with an air of defiance, or at least of contention. "Henrietta never told me she was writing to you," she said at last. "This is not kind of her."

"Is it so disagreeable to you to see me?" asked the young man.

"I didn't expect it. I don't like such surprises."

"But you knew I was in town; it was natural we should meet."

"Do you call this meeting? I hoped I shouldn't see you. In so big a place as London it seemed very possible."

"It was apparently repugnant to you even to write to me," her visitor went on.

Isabel made no reply; the sense of Henrietta Stackpole's treachery, as she momentarily qualified it, was strong within her. "Henrietta's certainly not a model of all the delicacies!" she exclaimed with bitterness. "It was a great liberty to take."

"I suppose I'm not a model either—of those virtues or of any others. The fault's mine as much as hers."

As Isabel looked at him it seemed to her that his jaw had never been more square. This might have displeased her, but she took a different turn. "No, it's not your fault so much as hers. What you've done was inevitable, I suppose, for you."

"It was indeed!" cried Caspar Goodwood with a voluntary laugh. "And now that I've come, at any rate, mayn't I stay?"

"You may sit down, certainly."

She went back to her chair again, while her visitor took the first place that offered, in the manner of a man accustomed to pay little thought to that sort of furtherance. "I've been hoping every day for an answer to my letter. You might have written me a few lines."

"It wasn't the trouble of writing that prevented me; I could as easily have written you four pages as one. But my silence was an intention," Isabel said. "I thought it the best thing."

He sat with his eyes fixed on hers while she spoke; then he lowered them and attached them to a spot in the carpet as if he were making a strong effort to say nothing but what he ought. He was a strong man in the wrong, and he was acute enough to see that an uncompromising exhibition of his strength would only throw the falsity of his position into relief. Isabel was not incapable of tasting any advantage of position over a person of this quality, and though little desirous to flaunt it in his face she could enjoy being able to say "You know you oughtn't to have written to me yourself!" and to say it with an air of triumph.

Caspar Goodwood raised his eyes to her own again; they seemed to shine through the vizard of a helmet. He had a strong sense of justice and was ready any day in the year—over and above this—to argue the question of his rights. "You said you hoped never to hear from me again; I know that. But I never accepted any such rule as my own. I warned you that you should hear very soon."

"I didn't say I hoped NEVER to hear from you," said Isabel.

"Not for five years then; for ten years; twenty years. It's the same thing."

"Do you find it so? It seems to me there's a great difference. I can imagine that at the end of ten years we might have a very pleasant correspondence. I shall have matured my epistolary style."

She looked away while she spoke these words, knowing them of so much less earnest a cast than the countenance of her listener. Her eyes, however, at last came back to him, just as he said very irrelevantly; "Are you enjoying your visit to your uncle?"

"Very much indeed." She dropped, but then she broke out. "What good do you expect to get by insisting?" "The good of not losing you."

"You've no right to talk of losing what's not yours. And even from your own point of view," Isabel added, "you ought to know when to let one alone."

"I disgust you very much," said Caspar Goodwood gloomily; not as if to provoke her to compassion for a man conscious of this blighting fact, but as if to set it well before himself, so that he might endeavour to act with his eyes on it.

"Yes, you don't at all delight me, you don't fit in, not in any way, just now, and the worst is that your putting it to the proof in this manner is quite unnecessary." It wasn't certainly as if his nature had been soft, so that pin-pricks would draw blood from it; and from the first of her acquaintance with him, and of her having to defend herself against a certain air that he had of knowing better what was good for her than she knew herself, she had recognised the fact that perfect frankness was her best weapon. To attempt to spare his sensibility or to escape from him edgewise, as one might do from a man who had barred the way less sturdily—this, in dealing with Caspar Goodwood, who would grasp at everything of every sort that one might give him, was wasted agility. It was not that he had not susceptibilities, but his passive surface, as well as his active, was large and hard, and he might always be trusted to dress his wounds, so far as they required it, himself. She came back, even for her measure of possible pangs and aches in him, to her old sense that he was naturally plated and steeled, armed essentially for aggression.

"I can't reconcile myself to that," he simply said. There was a dangerous liberality about it; for she felt how open it was to him to make the point that he had not always disgusted her.

"I can't reconcile myself to it either, and it's not the state of things that ought to exist between us. If you'd only try to banish me from your mind for a few months we should be on good terms again."

Novel Knowledge: SUPPORTIVE FRIENDS

Henry James and Edith Wharton supported each other as writers and friends. When she needed to complain about her marriage, he gave her encouraging words. When his publisher failed to pay him an advance for his novel *The Ivory Tower,* Edith secretly arranged for the publisher to pay him through her own money. James didn't need the money, but Edith felt it was terrible not to give such a fine writer his due.

"I see. If I should cease to think of you at all for a prescribed time, I should find I could keep it up indefinitely."

"Indefinitely is more than I ask. It's more even than I should like."

"You know that what you ask is impossible," said the young man, taking his adjective for granted in a manner she found irritating.

"Aren't you capable of making a calculated effort?" she demanded.

"You're strong for everything else; why shouldn't you be strong for that?"

"An effort calculated for what?" And then as she hung fire, "I'm capable of nothing with regard to you," he went on, "but just of being infernally in love with you. If one's strong one loves only the more strongly."

"There's a good deal in that;" and indeed our young lady felt the force of it—felt it thrown off, into the vast of truth and poetry, as practically a bait to her imagination. But she promptly came round.

"Think of me or not, as you find most possible; only leave me alone."

"Until when?"

"Well, for a year or two."

"Which do you mean? Between one year and two there's all the difference in the world."

"Call it two then," said Isabel with a studied effect of eagerness.

"And what shall I gain by that?" her friend asked with no sign of wincing.

"You'll have obliged me greatly."

"And what will be my reward?"

"Do you need a reward for an act of generosity?"

"Yes, when it involves a great sacrifice."

"There's no generosity without some sacrifice. Men don't understand such things. If you make the sacrifice you'll have all my admiration."

"I don't care a cent for your admiration—not one straw, with nothing to show for it. When will you marry me? That's the only question."

"Never—if you go on making me feel only as I feel at present."

"What do I gain then by not trying to make you feel otherwise?"

"You'll gain quite as much as by worrying me to death!" Caspar Goodwood bent his eyes again and gazed a while into the crown of his hat. A deep flush overspread his face; she could see her sharpness had at last penetrated. This immediately had a value—classic, romantic, redeeming, what did she know? for her; "the strong man in pain" was one of the categories of the human appeal, little charm as he might exert in the given case. "Why do you make me say such things to you?" she cried in a trembling voice. "I only want to be gentle—to be thoroughly kind. It's not delightful to me to feel people care for me and yet to have to try and reason them out of it. I think others also ought to be considerate; we have each to judge for ourselves. I know you're considerate, as much as you can be; you've good reasons for what you do. But I really don't want to marry, or to talk about it at all now. I shall probably never do it—no, never. I've a perfect right to feel that way, and it's no kindness to a woman to press her so hard, to urge her against her will. If I give you pain I can only say I'm very sorry. It's not my fault; I can't marry you simply to please you. I won't say that I shall always remain your friend, because when women say that, in these situations, it passes, I believe, for a sort of mockery. But try me some day."

Taylor Greer

IN *The Bean Trees* BY Barbara Kingsolver
First published in: 1988

Who is she? A gritty, sharp-witted Kentucky girl in search of something new.

Her Story

When Taylor Greer finally breaks out of Pittman, Kentucky, to explore the American West on her own, the last thing she wants is a baby. But that's what she gets. Not in the usual way, of course; the child is forced on Taylor in a parking lot. But that's not surprising. Nothing ever comes to Taylor in the usual way.

As Taylor begins to realize that this little girl has been abused, she decides not to drop the child off at the police station, but keeps traveling westbound with the baby in tow. She makes it as far as Arizona where she meets Mattie, owner of Jesus Is Lord Used Tire Store; LuAnne, a fellow Kentuckian; and two illegal immigrants. These people may be unlikely friends, but Taylor is the type of woman that good people gravitate to.

Taylor likes Arizona. Sort of. So, she decides to stick around a while and see what happens. However, it doesn't occur to her that she might fall in love with the little girl, until it's time to give her up. And she never imagines risking her own freedom to give an immigrant couple a chance at a new life in America until she has the opportunity to help. No, the things that happen to Taylor are not the things she imagined when she set out to explore the West. Still, it's hard to imagine she'd change any of her story—even if she could.

What Makes Taylor Greer So Memorable?

Marietta (Taylor) Greer is a gritty, young girl a few years out of high school. She decides to change her name from Marietta to Taylor while on this trip. What she lacks in money and opportunities she makes up for in guts, common sense, and the country charm she doesn't realize she has, "I feel like the only reason I have any friends at all is because I'm always careful not to say something totally dumb, and if I blow it just one time, then that's it." But of course, there are a lot of reasons why people like her. She has nerves of steel and a heart of gold. She's admirable, honest, and good in an old-fashioned, simple way. Don't expect her to show much affection, though. Taylor Greer is not the touchy-feely type.

The Life and Times of Barbara Kingsolver

Barbara Kingsolver spent some of her childhood years in Africa while her father was a doctor there, but most of her formative years were spent growing up in Carlisle, Kentucky. She credits her writing career to her rural upbringing; she watched practically no television and looked forward to visits from the bookmobile that came to town regularly. She studied piano at DePauw University in Indiana, but changed her major to biology. In the 1970s, after living in a number of places, she settled down in Tucson, Arizona, where she earned a master's degree in evolutionary biology and wrote for science journals and magazines.

In 1986, Kingsolver won the Arizona Press Club award for her feature writing. Two years later, she published *The Bean Trees*. Though she has lived most of her adult life in Tucson, Arizona, she along with her husband and two daughters packed up their lives in 2004 and moved to a farm in southwest Virginia.

FROM *The Bean Trees*

In our high school days the general idea of fun had been to paint "Class of '75" on the water tower, or maybe tie some farmer's goat up there on Halloween, but now I had serious intentions. In my first few years at Pittman County Hospital I was able to help Mama out with the rent and the bills and still managed to save up a couple hundred dollars. With most of it I bought a car, a '55 Volkswagen bug with no windows to speak of, and no back seat and no starter. But it was easy to push start without help once you got the hang of it, the wrong foot on the clutch and the other leg out the door, especially if you parked on a hill, which in that part of Kentucky you could hardly do anything but. In this car I intended to drive out of Pittman County one day and never look back, except maybe for Mama.

* * *

Novel Knowledge: LONG, LONELY NIGHTS

Kingsolver wrote *The Bean Trees* while pregnant and suffering from insomnia. To fill her long nights awake, she began writing the story of Taylor Greer. She finished the novel just before giving birth to her first child in March of 1987.

When I drove over the Pittman line I made two promises to myself. One I kept, the other I did not.

The first was that I would get myself a new name. I wasn't crazy about anything I had been called up to that point in life, and this seemed like the time to make a clean break. I didn't have any special name in mind, but just wanted a change. The more I thought about it, the more it seemed to me that a name is not something a person really has the right to pick out, but is something you're provided with more or less by chance. I decided to let the gas tank decide. Wherever it ran out, I'd look for a sign.

I came pretty close to being named after Homer, Illinois, but kept pushing it. I kept my fingers crossed through Sidney, Sadorus, Cerro Gordo, Decatur, and Blue Mound, and coasted into Taylorville on the fumes. And so I am Taylor Greer. I suppose you could say I had some part in choosing this name, but there was enough of destiny in it to satisfy me.

The second promise, the one that I broke, had to do with where I would end up. I had looked at some maps, but since I had never in my own memory been outside of Kentucky (I was evidently born in Cincinnati, but that is beside the point), I had no way of knowing why or how any particular place might be preferable to any other. That is, apart from the pictures on the gas station brochures: Tennessee claimed to be the Volunteer State, and Missouri the Show-Me State, whatever that might mean, and nearly everyplace appeared to have plenty of ladies in fifties hairdos standing near waterfalls. These brochures I naturally did not trust as far as I could throw them out the window. Even Pittman, after all, had once been chosen an All-Kentucky City, on the basis of what I do not know. Its abundance of potato bugs and gossip, perhaps. I knew how people could toot their own horn without any earthly cause.

And so what I promised myself is that I would drive west until my car stopped running, and there I would stay. But there were some things I hadn't considered. Mama taught me well about tires, and many other things besides, but I knew nothing of rocker arms. And I did not know about the Great Plain.

The sight of it filled me with despair. I turned south from Wichita, Kansas, thinking I might find a way around it, but I didn't. There was central Oklahoma. I had never imagined that any part of a round earth could be so flat. In Kentucky you could never see too far, since there were always mountains blocking the other side of your view, and it left you the chance to think something good might be just over the next hill. But out there on the plain it was all laid out right in front of you, and no matter how far you looked it didn't get any better. Oklahoma made me feel there was nothing left to hope for.

Novel Knowledge: SUCCESS THROUGH WORD-OF-MOUTH

Since *The Bean Trees* was Kingsolver's first book, a modest number of copies were printed. However, as the life and times of Taylor Greer spread by word-of-mouth, demand for the book grew. The novel has been continuously in print ever since and has been translated into 12 languages.

My car gave out somewhere in the middle of a great emptiness that according to the road signs was owned by the Cherokee tribe. Suddenly the steering wheel bore no relation to where the car was going. By the grace of some miracle I surely did not yet deserve, I managed to wobble off the highway all in one piece and find a service station.

The man who straightened out my rocker arm was named Bob Two Two. I am not saying he didn't ask for a fair price—I should have been able to fix it myself—but he went home that night with his pocket full of something near half the money I had. I sat in the parking lot looking out over that godless stretch of nothing and came the closest I have ever come to cashing in and plowing under. But there was no sense in that. My car was fixed.

I had to laugh, really. All my life, Mama had talked about the Cherokee Nation as our ace in the hole. She'd had an old grandpa that was full-blooded Cherokee, one of the few that got left behind in Tennessee because he was too old or too ornery to get marched over to Oklahoma. Mama would say, "If we run out of luck we can always go live on the Cherokee Nation." She and I both had enough blood to qualify. According to Mama, if you're one-eighth or more they let you in. She called this our "head rights."

Of course, if she had ever been there she would have known it was not a place you'd ever go to live without some kind of lethal weapon aimed at your hind end. It was clear to me that the whole intention of bringing the Cherokees here was to get them to lie down and die without a fight. The Cherokees believed God was in trees. Mama told me this. When I was a kid I would climb as high as I could in a tree and not come down until dinner. "That's your Indian blood," she would say. "You're trying to see God."

From what I could see, there was not one tree in the entire state of Oklahoma.

The sun was headed fast for the flat horizon, and then there would be nothing but twelve hours of headlights in front of me. I was in a hurry to get out of there. My engine was still running from Bob Two Two's jumper cables, and I hated to let a good start go to waste, but I was tired and didn't want to begin a night of driving without a cup of coffee and something to eat. I drove across the big patch of dirt that lay between the garage and another small brick-shaped building that had a neon Budweiser light in the window.
* * *

The air was cool and I drank it too fast, getting a little dizzy. I sat with my hands on the steering wheel for a few minutes trying to think myself into the right mood for driving all night across Oklahoma.

I jumped when she pecked on the windshield. It was the round woman in the blanket.

"No thanks," I said. I thought she wanted to wash the windshield, but instead she went around to the other side and opened the door. "You need a lift someplace?" I asked her.

Her body, her face, and her eyes were all round. She was someone you could have drawn a picture of by tracing around dimes and quarters and jar tops. She opened up the blanket and took out something alive. It was a child. She wrapped her blanket around and around it until it became a round bundle with a head. Then she set this bundle down on the seat of my car.

"Take this baby," she said.

It wasn't a baby, exactly. It was probably old enough to walk, though not so big that it couldn't be easily carried. Somewhere between a baby and a person.

"Where do you want me to take it?"

She looked back at the bar, and then looked at me. "Just take it."

I waited a minute, thinking that soon my mind would clear and I would understand what she was saying. It didn't. The child had the exact same round eyes. All four of those eyes were hanging there in the darkness, hanging on me, waiting. The Budweiser sign blinked on and off, on and off, throwing a faint light that made the whites of their eyes look orange.

"Is this your kid?"

She shook her head. "My dead sister's."

"Are you saying you want to give me this child?"

"Yes."

"If I wanted a baby I would have stayed in Kentucky," I informed her. "I could have had babies coming out my ears by now."

A man came out of the bar, gray hat or brown hat I couldn't tell because my car was parked some distance from the door. He got into a pickup truck but didn't start the ignition or turn on the lights.

"Is that your man in there, in the bar?" I asked her.

"Don't go back in there. I'm not saying why. Just don't."

"Look," I said, "even if you wanted to, you can't just give somebody a kid. You got to have the papers and stuff. Even a car has papers, to prove you didn't steal it."

"This baby's got no papers. There isn't nobody knows it's alive, or cares. Nobody that matters, like the police or nothing like that. This baby was born in a Plymouth."

"Well, it didn't happen this morning," I said. "Plymouth or no Plymouth, this child has been around long enough for somebody to notice." I had a foggy understanding that I wasn't arguing the right point. This was getting us nowhere.

She put her hands where the child's shoulders might be, under all that blanket, and pushed it gently back into the seat, trying to make it belong there. She looked at it for a long time. Then she closed the door and walked away.

As I watched her I was thinking that she wasn't really round. Without the child and the blanket she walked away from my car a very thin woman.

I held the steering wheel and dug my fingernails into my palms, believing the pain might force my brain to wake up and think what to do. While I was thinking, the woman got in the pickup truck and it drove away without lights.

Rachel

IN *MADEMOISELLE FIFI* BY GUY DE MAUPASSANT

FIRST PUBLISHED IN: 1882

Who is she? A proud French Jewish prostitute who fights back in the face of defeat.

Her Story

Rachel may be a prostitute, but she is no ordinary whore. She's willing to sell her body, but not her mind. In fact, her outspoken nature surprises a group of Prussians who have gone to Paris to round up prostitutes for soldiers in Normandy to enjoy.

Rachel, the smallest prostitute in the bunch, is paired up with Wilhelm, a soldier nicknamed Mademoiselle Fifi due to his small stature and feminine manner. The little soldier with his loud mouth, filthy jokes, and girlish gestures repulses Rachel. She lets him run his cold hands over her body and bite into her skin until she bleeds, but she won't let him get away with insulting France. When he announces to the whole crowd at a dinner, "the women of France belong to us!" Rachel shouts back and challenges him. He laughs and reminds her that she is at this dinner to serve him. "I, I, I am not a woman! I am a prostitute! And that is all a Prussian deserves!" Embarrassed, Fifi slaps her hard across the face. Without blinking, Rachel grabs a knife from the table and stabs the nasty little solider in the neck. She runs away while everyone is in shock. Mademoiselle Fifi dies. And the hunt is on for Rachel.

What Makes Rachel So Memorable?

Rachel is a small, feisty, Jewish prostitute in 1870s France during the Prussian war. Everything from her hair to the way she walks into a room is striking but it's her attitude and the way she boldly says exactly what she thinks that makes a lasting impression. Whether the impression is good or bad depends on your own views, but Rachel doesn't care. She represents her country with her dignity and defiance in the face of defeat. She is proud and unyielding. And if all of that isn't enough to make her memorable, she kills a man and gets away with it.

The Life and Times of Guy de Maupassant

In 1869, when Guy de Maupassant was nineteen, he quit studying law in Paris and left home to fight in the Franco-Prussian War. Between 1872 and 1880, he worked at the ministry of maritime affairs, then at the ministry of education. In 1880, he published his first collection of poems, followed by more than three hundred short stories, six novels, three travelogues, and a collection called *Boule De Suif* ("Ball of Fat"). Maupassant suffered from syphilis throughout his twenties, and the disease is believed to have caused his mental problems. In 1892, when he was forty-two, Maupassant tried to kill himself by cutting his throat. He was committed to an insane asylum in Paris and died there one year later.

From *Mademoiselle Fifi*

Notwithstanding the rain, the window was kept open and from time to time one of them went over to listen. At ten minutes past six o'clock, the Baron reported a distant rolling. They all hurried downstairs, and soon the large carriage came up with the four horses still galloping, covered with mud up to their backs, steaming and blowing.

And five women got off the carriage and stepped on the perron, five graceful girls carefully selected by a chum of the Captain, to whom Pflicht had taken a card from his officer.

> *Novel Knowledge:* LEARNED FROM THE BEST
>
> When Maupassant's mother saw the talent for writing her son possessed she arranged for him to learn more about writing from Gustave Flaubert, author of *Madame Bovary*. Flaubert was a huge influence on Maupassant.

They had not been reluctant to come, knowing that they would be well paid; besides, they were quite well acquainted and familiar with the Prussians, having been in intercourse with them for the past three months and making the best of men as of things. "Our business requires it," they told each other on their way, no doubt in order to ease off some secret pricking of a remnant of conscience.

And, presently, they were ushered into the dining-room. Lighted up, the dining-room looked still more lugubrious in its pitiful dilapidation, and the table covered with viands, rich china and silver plate, which had been discovered in the wall where the owner had hidden them, gave to the premises the appearance of a low tavern, where bandits are having supper after a successful raffle. The Captain, radiant, took hold of the women as of a familiar thing, appreciating them, embracing them, scenting them, estimating them at their value as instruments of pleasure; and as the three younger men wanted to take one each, he objected to it with authority, reserving to himself the privilege of making the assignments, in perfect fairness, according to rank, so as not to injure in any way the hierarchy.

Then, in order to preclude any discussion, any contest and any suspicion of partiality, he lined them up according to height, and addressing the tallest, in a tone of command: "Your name?"

She replied, raising her voice: "Pamela."

Then he announced: "Number one, by the name of Pamela, is adjudged to the Commander."

Having then kissed Blondine, the second as a mark of his claim to ownership, he offered the fat Amanda to Lieutenant Otto; Eva la Tomate to Second-Lieutenant Fritz, and the smallest of all, Rachel, a very young brunette, with black eyes like ink spots, a Jewess whose pug nose confirmed the rule that ascribes hooked noses to all her race, to the youngest officer, the frail Markgraf Wilhelm von Eyrik.

As a matter of fact they were all pretty and plump, without any distinctive character on their faces, shaped almost alike in appearance and style and complexion by the daily practice of their illicit trade and the life in common in disreputable houses.

The three young men wanted immediately to take their partners out of the room under pretext of offering them brushes and soap for washing and freshening up; but the Captain was wise enough not to allow it, claiming that they were clean enough to sit down to dinner, and for fear that those who went up might want to change their girls when they came down, and thus disturb the other couples. His experience prevailed. There were only plenty of kisses, kisses of expectancy.

Suddenly Rachel suffocated, coughing to tears and rejecting smoke through her nose. The Markgraf, feigning to kiss her, had blown a whiff of tobacco into her mouth. She did not get angry, did not utter a single word, but glared at her possessor with anger aroused way down at the bottom of her black eyes.

They sat down to dinner. The Commander himself seemed to be delighted; he took Pamela on his right and Blondine on his left, and while unfolding his napkin, he declared:—"This was a charming idea of yours, Captain!"

Novel Knowledge: WARTIME PROPAGANDA

While the original *Mademoiselle Fifi* story was set during the Franco-Prussian War, the movie adaptation was allied propaganda clearly aimed at confronting the German occupation of World War II.

Lieutenants Otto and Fritz, polite and obsequious as if they were sitting near Society ladies, did slightly intimidate their neighbors; but Baron von Kelweingstein, let loose in his vice, was beaming; he cracked unsavory jokes, and with his crown of red hair, seemed to be on fire. He paid gallant compliments in his defective French of the Rhine, and his lewd nonsense, smacking of taverns, expectorated through the hole between his two broken teeth, reached the girls in the middle of a rapid fire of saliva.

The girls did not understand his witticisms, and their intelligence did not seem to be awakened until he sputtered obscene words, rough expressions, crippled by his accent. Then all in a chorus began to laugh as if they were demented, falling on the laps of their neighbors, repeating the words which the Baron disfigured purposely in order to make them say filthy things. They vomited at will plenty of them, intoxicated after drinking from the first bottles of wine; and relapsing into their real selves, opening the gates to their habits, they kissed mustaches on their right and those on their left, pinched arms, uttered furious screams, drank out of all the glasses, sang French couplets and bits of German songs they had learned in their daily intercourse with the enemy.

Soon the men themselves flushed and excited by the female flesh spread under their nose and within reach of their hands, lost all restraint, roaring, breaking the plates, while behind them impassive soldiers were waiting.

The Commander only kept some restraint.

Mademoiselle Fifi had taken Rachel on his knees and deliberately working himself up to a pitch of frenzy, kissed madly the ebony curls on her neck, inhaling through the thin interstice between the gown and her skin, the sweet warmth of her body and the full fragrance of her person; through the silk, he pinched her furiously making her scream, seized with a rabid ferocity and distracted by his craving for destruction. Often also holding her in his arms, squeezing her as if he wanted to mix her with himself, he pressed long kisses on the fresh lips of the Jewess and embraced her until he lost breath; but suddenly he bit her so deep that a dash of blood flowed down the chin of the young girl and ran into her waist.

Once more she looked at him, straight in the face, and washing the wound, she muttered: "You will have to pay for it!" He began to laugh, with a harsh laugh: "All right, I shall pay!" said he.

At dessert, champagne was served. The Commander rose and with the same tone as he would have taken to drink the health of the Empress Augusta, he said:

"To our ladies!" And a series of toasts were then drunk, toasts with the gallantry and manner of drunkards and troopers, mixed with obscene jokes, rendered still more brutal by their ignorance of the language.

They were rising one after the other, trying to be witty, making efforts to be funny; and the women, so intoxicated that they were hardly able to sit up, with their vacant look, their heavy, clammy tongues, applauded vociferously each time.

The Captain, no doubt intending to lend the orgy an atmosphere of gallantry, raised once more his glass and pronounced: "To our victories over the hearts!"

Then Lieutenant Otto, a kind of bear from the Black Forest, jumped up, inflamed, saturated with drinks, and suddenly, carried away by alcoholic patriotism, he cried: "To our victories over France!"

Intoxicated as they were, the women kept silent and Rachel, shuddering with rage, retorted: "Well! I know some Frenchmen in whose presence you would not dare say such things."

But the little Markgraf, still holding her on his knees, began to laugh, having become exceedingly exhilarated by the wine: "Ah! Ah! Ah! I never met any myself. As soon as they see us, they run away."

The girl exasperated, shouted in his face: "You lie, you dirty pig!"

For a second he fixed on her his clear eyes, as he used to fix them on the paintings the canvas of which he riddled with revolver shots; then he laughed: "Oh yes! let us speak of it, you beauty! Would we be here if they were brave?"—and he became more and more excited: "We are their masters; France belongs to us!"

She sprang off his knees and fell back on her chair. He rose, held out his glass over the table and repeated: "France, the French, their fields, their woods and their houses belong to us!"

The others, who were thoroughly intoxicated, suddenly shaken by military enthusiasm, the enthusiasm of brutes, seized their glasses and shouted vociferously: "Long live Prussia!" and emptied them at a draught.

The girls did not protest, reduced to silence and frightened. Even Rachel kept silent, unable to reply.

Then the little Markgraf placed on the head of the Jewess his glass of Champaign, refilled, and said—"The women of France belong to us!"

She jumped up so quickly that the glass was upset and spilled the yellow wine in her black hair, as for a baptism; it fell broken to pieces on the floor. Her lips quivering, she looked defiantly at the officer; the latter kept laughing; she stammered in a voice choked with rage: "That, that is not true! you shall never have the women of France!"

He sat down to laugh at his ease and tried to imitate the Parisian accent: "That is a good one! that is a good one! And what are you doing here, you little one?"

Confused, at first, she did not answer, as she did not, in her excitement, understand fully what he said; then, as soon as the meaning of it dawned on her mind, she shouted at him indignantly and vehemently: "I, I, I am not a woman! I am a prostitute! And that is all a Prussian deserves!"

Hardly had she finished, that he slapped her face violently; but, as he was raising his hand again, maddened with rage she caught on the table a small silver-bladed dessert knife, and so quickly that nobody noticed it, she stabbed him right in the neck, just at the hollow where the breast begins.

A word, that he was about to mutter, was cut short in his throat, and he remained stiff, with his mouth open and a frightful look.

All shouted and got up tumultuously; but having thrown her chair in the legs of Lieutenant Otto, who collapsed and fell down at full length, she ran to the window, opened it before they could catch her, and jumped out in the night, under the rain that was still falling.

Scarlett O'Hara

IN *GONE WITH THE WIND* BY MARGARET MITCHELL
FIRST PUBLISHED IN: 1936

Who is she? A ruthless woman who does whatever needs to be done to save her home, her family, and most of all herself.

Her Story

Before the Civil War, Scarlett O'Hara is little more than a spoiled teenage Southern belle. She pines over the boy next door, and frets over how many boys will sit around her at a family barbecue. But when Scarlett sees the horrors the war brings, her carefree life begins to fade. Yankee soldiers attack her home and family, her mother dies, her father loses his mind, and her sisters prove useless and weak. Throughout all this chaos, Scarlett emerges as a leader for the O'Hara family. She does whatever needs to be done in order to get through each day. Her self-centered nature, once a vice, is now a virtue that serves her well.

After the war—after she has nearly starved to death, worked the fields in the hot Georgia sun, and shot a Yankee dead—Scarlett finds she cannot go back to a life of leisure. She can still charm the men, but now she always has a selfish motive.

Scarlett's counterpart throughout the novel is Rhett Butler, a wealthy man who likes Scarlett's selfish and feisty ways. She reminds him a lot of himself. Before, during, and after the war, Rhett is nearby and Scarlett always manages to find him when she needs him. He isn't fooled for a second by the way she plays a good-natured, Southernbelle, but he still finds her irresistible. Rhett is the only man who sees Scarlett for what she really is—and loves her anyway. Of all the men she has ever known, there has never been anyone quite like him, and Scarlett doesn't know whether to love him or hate him.

What Makes Scarlett O'Hara So Memorable?

Scarlett O'Hara does whatever has to be done period. Plain and simple. She marries one man out of spite. She marries another to pay her property taxes. And she shoots a man when she hears him walking into her kitchen; after all the hard work she put into that meal, no Yankee was going to eat it! Instead of staying with her family in Atlanta, Scarlett decides to stay on her family's plantation to face down anyone who would take it away from her. Those who try always end up regretting it. Arguably the most unforgettable woman in fiction, Scarlett may be the most strong-willed and ruthless character ever created.

The Life and Times of Margaret Mitchell

Margaret Mitchell was among the first female columnists to write for the South's largest paper, the *Atlanta Journal*. Born and raised in Atlanta, Georgia, most of her columns had to do with the South's elite and their trips abroad, but Mitchell was always interested in the South's history—particularly the Civil War.

In 1922, Mitchell married Berrien "Red" Upshaw, but the marriage ended in divorce when she found out about his bootlegging. John Marsh had been Upshaw's best man in their wedding, but turned out to be a better husband for Mitchell.

When she broke her ankle in 1926, John brought home a stack of historical books from the library. He also suggested that she try her hand at writing a novel while she was stuck at home, so she started writing *Gone with the Wind*. Her ankle healed, but she kept writing. By chance, she had the opportunity to meet Macmillan editor Harold

Latham while he was in Atlanta. He had read her columns and liked her personally. Once she showed him the manuscript he was quick to make her an offer. Mitchell enjoyed the book's success for more than a decade but, in 1949, while she and John were on their way to see a film, a drunk driver struck their car. After five days in the hospital, Mitchell died.

FROM *Gone with the Wind*

Scarlett sat on a high rosewood ottoman, under the shade of a huge oak in the rear of the house, her flounces and ruffles billowing about her and two inches of green morocco slippers—all that a lady could show and still remain a lady—peeping from beneath them. She had a scarcely touched plate in her hands and seven cavaliers about her. The barbecue had reached its peak and the warm air was full of laughter and talk, the click of silver on porcelain and the rich heavy smells of roasting meats and redolent gravies. Occasionally when the slight breeze veered, puffs of smoke from the long barbecue pits floated over the crowd and were greeted with squeals of mock dismay from the ladies and violent flappings of palmetto fans.

Novel Knowledge: ECHOES OF POETRY

The novel's title comes from a poem by Ernest Dowson. Scarlett says this phrase when her home is overtaken by the Yankees and she wonders if the plantation and way of life is "also gone with the wind which had swept through Georgia."

Most of the young ladies were seated with partners on the long benches that faced the tables, but Scarlett, realizing that a girl has only two sides and only one man can sit on each of these sides, had elected to sit apart so she could gather about her as many men as possible.

* * *

The bright sunlight in the front yard suddenly clouded and the trees blurred through tears. Scarlett dropped her head on her arms and struggled not to cry. Crying was so useless now. The only time crying ever did any good was when there was a man around from whom you wished favors. As she crouched there, squeezing her eyes tightly to keep back the tears, she was startled by the sound of trotting hooves. But she did not raise her head. She had imagined that sound too often in the nights and days of these last two weeks, just as she had imagined she heard the rustle of Ellen's skirts. Her heart hammered, as it always did at such moments before she told herself sternly: "Don't be a fool."

Novel Knowledge: $47.00 A COPY

Gone with the Wind was published in 1936 at the unprecedented price of $3.00 (equal to $47.00 today). In less than six months, over one million copies were sold. Despite its 1,019 pages, people couldn't put the book down.

But the hooves slowed down in a startlingly natural way to the rhythm of a walk and there was the measured scrunch-scrunch on the gravel. It was a horse—the Tartletons, the Fontaines! She looked up quickly. It was a Yankee cavalryman.

Automatically, she dodged behind the curtain and peered fascinated at him through the dim folds of the cloth, so startled that the breath went out of her lungs with a gasp.

He sat slouched in the saddle, a thick, rough-looking man with an unkempt black beard straggling over his unbuttoned blue jacket. Little close-set eyes, squinting in the sun glare, calmly surveyed the house from beneath the visor of his tight blue cap. As he slowly dismounted and tossed the bridle reins over the hitching post, Scarlett's breath came back to her as suddenly and painfully as after a blow in the stomach. A Yankee, a Yankee with a long pistol on his hip! And she was alone in the house with three sick girls and the babies!

As he lounged up the walk, hand on holster, beady little eyes glancing to right and left, a kaleidoscope of jumbled pictures spun in her mind, stories Aunt Pittypat had whispered of attacks on unprotected women, throat cuttings, houses burned over the heads of dying women, children bayoneted because they cried, all of the unspeakable horrors that lay bound up in the name of "Yankee."

Her first terrified impulse was to hide in the closet, crawl under the bed, fly down the back stairs and run screaming to the swamp, anything to escape him. Then she heard his cautious feet on the front steps and his stealthy tread as he entered the hall and she knew that escape was cut off. Too cold with fear to move, she heard his progress from room to room downstairs, his steps growing louder and bolder as he discovered no one. Now he was in the dining room and in a moment he would walk out into the kitchen.

At the thought of the kitchen, rage suddenly leaped up in Scarlett's breast, so sharply that it jabbed at her heart like a knife thrust, and fear fell away before her overpowering fury. The kitchen! There, over the open kitchen fire were two pots, one filled with apples stewing and the other with a hodgepodge of vegetables brought painfully from Twelve Oaks and the MacIntosh garden—dinner that must serve for nine hungry people and hardly enough for two. Scarlett had been restraining her appetite for hours, waiting for the return of the others and the thought of the Yankee eating their meager meal made her shake with anger.

God damn them all! They descended like locusts and left Tara to starve slowly and now they were back again to steal the poor leavings. Her empty stomach writhed within her. By God, this was one Yankee who would do no more stealing!

She slipped off her worn shoe and, barefooted, she pattered swiftly to the bureau, not even feeling her festered toe. She opened the top drawer soundlessly and caught up the heavy pistol she had brought from Atlanta, the weapon Charles had worn but never fired. She fumbled in the leather box that hung on the wall below his saber and brought out a cap. She slipped it into place with a hand that did not shake. Quickly and noiselessly, she ran into the upper hall and down the stairs, steadying herself on the banisters with one hand and holding the pistol close to her thigh in the folds of her skirt.

"Who's there?" cried a nasal voice and she stopped on the middle of the stairs, the blood thudding in her ears so loudly she could hardly hear him. "Halt or I'll shoot!" came the voice.

He stood in the door of the dining room, crouched tensely, his pistol in one hand and, in the other, the small rosewood sewing box fitted with gold thimble, gold-handled scissors and tiny gold-topped acorn of emery. Scarlett's legs felt cold to the knees but rage scorched her face. Ellen's sewing box in his hands. She wanted to cry: "Put it down! Put it down, you dirty—" but the words would not come. She could only stare over the banisters at him and watch his face change from harsh tenseness to a half-contemptuous, half-ingratiating smile.

"So there is somebody ter home," he said, slipping his pistol back into its holster and moving into the hall until he stood directly below her. "All alone, little lady?"

Like lightning, she shoved her weapon over the banisters and into the startled bearded face. Before he could even fumble at his belt, she pulled the trigger. The back kick of the pistol made her reel, as the roar of the explosion filled her ears and the acrid smoke stung her nostrils. The man crashed backwards to the floor, sprawling into the dining room with a violence that shook the furniture. The box clattered from his hand, the contents spilling about him. Hardly aware that she was moving, Scarlett ran down the stairs and stood over him, gazing down into what was left of the face above the beard, a bloody pit where the nose had been, glazing eyes burned with powder. As she looked, two streams of blood crept across the shining floor, one from his face and one from the back of his head.

Yes, he was dead. Undoubtedly. She had killed a man.

Sula Peace

IN *SULA* BY TONI MORRISON

FIRST PUBLISHED IN: 1973

Who is she? An unpredictable woman who raises doubts about the meaning of right and wrong.

Her Story

Sula Peace thinks women, especially friends, should share their men. It's no wonder she thinks this way. Her mother, Hannah, and her grandmother have men coming and going from the house all the time, men who are the fathers of Sula's schoolgirl friends. Her mother has only one rule—men don't stay overnight. (That would be too personal.) Sula grows up with these women in a house on a hill in Medallion, Ohio, referred to as "the Bottom," and it is because of these women that she forms a lot of unusual ideas about relationships with both men and women.

While still a little girl, Sula meets Nel Wright and the two quickly become best friends. Their bond grows even stronger when tragedy strikes and they decide to keep a terrible secret between them. Once grown, Sula leaves the Bottom in search of excitement, while Nel stays behind, marries, and raises a family. Eventually, Sula decides that people live the same dull existence everywhere, so she may as well go back to Medallion. But when she returns, she is greeted with suspicion and whispers. Folks assume she's been up to no good all these years. She is, after all, her mother's daughter. The only one happy to see Sula is Nel. For Nel, "Talking to Sula had always been a conversation with herself." But Sula does the unforgivable when she sleeps with Nel's husband. Suddenly, everything that bonded them over the years begins to unravel.

What Makes Sula Peace So Memorable?

There is nothing ordinary about Sula. Molded by the strange and elusive ways of her mother and grandmother, she sees the world through unconventional eyes and often without any appearance of feelings. As a child Sula cuts her own finger with a sharp knife to scare off a pack of mean boys. They watch the blood run down her hand and she tells them, "If I can do that to myself, what you suppose I'll do to you?" As a woman, her actions and her reactions are no less shocking and no easier to predict. But Sula is more than a story of a woman who lives by her own code. She manages to shake our confidence and cause us to wonder if we really know the difference between right and wrong. Spend enough time with Sula and you just might begin to question everything you thought you knew about good and evil.

The Life and Times of Toni Morrison

Nobel Prize–winning American author Toni Morrison has come a long way from her working-class roots in Lorain, Ohio. She graduated from Howard University in 1953, and after earning a Master's Degree in English from Cornell she returned to Howard University to teach. In 1958, she married Harold Morrison, a Jamaican architect and fellow faculty member. They had two children, but divorced in 1964. With children in tow, Toni moved to Syracuse, New York, and worked as a textbook editor before landing a book-editing position at Random House. In 1970, she published her first novel, *The Bluest Eye*. Literary critics loved it, but sales were modest. Her second novel, *Sula*, came three years later, and she won the Pulitzer Prize for her third novel, *Beloved*, in 1988. From 1989 to 2006, Morrison taught at Princeton. In 1993, she received the Nobel Prize for literature. Morrison, arguably among the most gifted writers living today, continues to write some of America's most subtle, yet unnerving novels.

FROM *Sula*

Her old friend had come home. Sula. Who made her laugh, who made her see old things with new eyes, in whose presence she felt clever, gentle and a little raunchy. Sula, whose past she had lived through and with whom the present was a constant sharing of perceptions. Talking to Sula had always been a conversation with herself. Was there anyone else before whom she could never be foolish? In whose view inadequacy was mere idiosyncrasy, a character trait rather than a deficiency? Anyone who left behind that aura of fun and complicity? Sula never competed; she simply helped others define themselves. Other people seemed to turn their volume on and up when Sula was in the room. More than any other thing, humor returned. She could listen to the crunch of sugar underfoot that the children had spilled without reaching for the switch; and she forgot the tear in the living-room window shade. Even Nel's love for Jude, which over the years had spun a steady gray web around her heart, became a bright and easy affection, a playfulness that was reflected in their lovemaking.

Sula would come by of an afternoon, walking along with her fluid stride, wearing a plain yellow dress the same way her mother, Hannah, had worn those too-big house dresses—with a distance, an absence of a relationship to clothes which emphasized everything the fabric covered. When she scratched the screen door, as in the old days, and stepped inside, the dishes piled in the sink looked as though they belonged there; the dust on the lamps sparkled; the hair brush lying on the "good" sofa in the living room did not have to be apologetically retrieved, and Nel's grimy intractable children looked like three wild things happily insouciant in the May shine.

"Hey, girl." The rose mark over Sula's eye gave her glance a suggestion of startled pleasure. It was darker than Nel remembered.

"Hey yourself. Come on in here."

"How you doin'?" Sula moved a pile of ironed diapers from a chair and sat down.

"Oh, I ain't strangled nobody yet so I guess I'm all right."

"Well, if you change your mind call me."

"Somebody need killin'?"

"Half this town need it."

"And the other half?"

"A drawn-out disease."

"Oh, come on. Is Medallion that bad?"

"Didn't nobody tell you?"

"You been gone too long, Sula."

"Not too long, but maybe too far."

* * *

She came to their church suppers without underwear, bought their steaming platters of food and merely picked at it—relishing nothing, exclaiming over no one's ribs or cobbler. They believed that she was laughing at their God.

And the fury she created in the women of the town was incredible—for she would lay their husbands once and then no more. Hannah had been a nuisance, but she was complimenting the women, in a way, by wanting their husbands. Sula was trying them out and discarding them without any excuse the men could swallow. So the women, to justify their own judgment, cherished their men more, soothed the pride and vanity Sula had bruised.

Novel Knowledge: OPRAH WINFREY CHOOSES *SULA*

In 1973, *Sula* was critically acclaimed as a superb follow-up to Morrison's literary debut *The Bluest Eye*. In 2002, *Sula* gained a new fan—Oprah Winfrey. With a much larger audience, the novel served as a spotlight on the struggles in friendships between childhood girls as they grow to be women.

Among the weighty evidence piling up was the fact that Sula did not look her age. She was near thirty and, unlike them, had lost no teeth, suffered no bruises, developed no ring of fat at the waist or pocket at the back of her neck. It was rumored that she had had no childhood diseases, was never known to have chicken pox, croup or even a runny nose. She had played rough as a child—where were the scars? Except for a funny-shaped finger and that evil birthmark, she was free of any normal signs of vulnerability. Some of the men, who as boys had dated her, remembered that on picnics neither gnats nor mosquitoes would settle on her. Patsy, Hannah's one-time friend, agreed and said not only that, but she had witnessed the fact that when Sula drank beer she never belched . . .

They would no more run Sula out of town than they would kill the robins that brought her back, for in their secret awareness of Him, He was not the God of three faces they sang about. They knew quite well that He had four, and that the fourth explained Sula. They had lived with various forms of evil all their days, and it wasn't that they believed God would take care of them. It was rather that they knew God had a brother and that brother hadn't spared God's son, so why should he spare them?

There was no creature so ungodly as to make them destroy it. They could kill easily if provoked to anger, but not by design, which explained why they could not "mob kill" anyone. To do so was not only unnatural, it was undignified. The presence of evil was something to be first recognized, then dealt with, survived, outwitted, triumphed over.

Their evidence against Sula was contrived, but their conclusions about her were not. Sula was distinctly different. Eva's arrogance and Hannah's self-indulgence merged in her and, with a twist that was all her own imagination, she lived out her days exploring her own thoughts and emotions, giving them full reign, feeling no obligation to please anybody unless their pleasure pleased her. As willing to feel pain as to give pain, to feel pleasure as to give pleasure, hers was an experimental life—ever since her mother's remarks sent her flying up those stairs, ever since her one major feeling of responsibility had been exorcised on the bank of a river with a closed place in the middle. The first experience taught her there was no other that you could count on; the second that there was no self to count on either. She had no center, no speck around which to grow. In the midst of a pleasant conversation with someone she might say, "Why do you chew with your mouth open?" not because the answer interested her but because she wanted to see the person's face change rapidly. She was completely free of ambition, with no affection for money, property or things, no greed, no desire to command attention or compliments—no ego. For that reason she felt no compulsion to verify herself—be consistent with herself.

Novel Knowledge: A Guest at the Louvre

In 2006, Morrison was invited to the Louvre Museum in Paris as its second "Grand Invité." The theme of the program was "The Foreigner's Home." Morrison was so inspired by the event that she returned to Princeton and created a seminar with the same theme.

She had clung to Nel as the closest thing to both an other and a self, only to discover that she and Nel were not one and the same thing. She had no thought at all of causing Nel pain when she bedded down with Jude. They had always shared the affection of other people: compared how a boy kissed, what line he used with one and then the other. Marriage, apparently, had changed all that, but having had no intimate knowledge of marriage, having lived in a house with women who thought all men available, and selected from among them with a care only for their tastes, she was ill prepared for the possessiveness of the one person she felt close to. She knew well enough what other women said and felt, or said they felt. But she and Nel had always seen through them. They both knew that those women were not jealous of other women; that they were only afraid of losing their jobs. Afraid their husbands would discover that no uniqueness lay between their legs . . .

It has surprised her a little and saddened her a good deal when Nel behaved the way the others would have. Nel was one of the reasons she had drifted back to Medallion, that and the boredom she found in Nashville, Detroit, New Orleans, New York, Philadelphia, Macon and San Diego. All those cities held the same people, working the same mouths, sweating the same sweat. The men who took her to one or another of those places had merged into one large personality: the same language of love, the same entertainments of love, the same cooling of love. Whenever she introduced her private thoughts into their rubbings or goings, they hooded their eyes. They taught her nothing but love tricks, shared nothing but worry, gave nothing but money. She had been looking all along for a friend, and it took her a while to discover that a lover was not a comrade and could never be—for a woman. And that no one would ever be that version of herself which she sought to reach out to and touch with an ungloved hand. There was only her own mood and whim, and if that was all there was, she decided to turn the naked hand toward it, discover it and let others become as intimate with their own selves as she was.

In a way, her strangeness, her naïveté, her craving for the other half of her equation was the consequence of an idle imagination. Had she paints, or clay, or knew the discipline of the dance, or strings; had she anything to engage her tremendous curiosity and her gift for metaphor, she might have exchanged the restlessness and preoccupation with whim for an activity that provided her with all she yearned for. And like any artist with no art form, she became dangerous.

Roxane Coss

IN *Bel Canto* BY ANN PATCHETT

FIRST PUBLISHED IN: 2001

Who is she? A privileged but gutsy opera singer comes to terms with the hostage situation she finds herself in.

Her Story

Roxane Coss is often referred to as simply "The Soprano." A native of Chicago, she grew up to become a world-renowned opera singer. Her voice has allowed her to perform in the finest opera houses and theaters. Her voice has also brought her a lot of money and allowed her to avoid the mundane things in life such as waiting in lines. Unfortunately, nothing—not even her beautiful singing voice—can help her when she, along with fifty-eight other people, is taken hostage. She was performing at the home of the vice president of a South American country (the exact country is never named) for the birthday of a wealthy Japanese man named Hosokawa when terrorists crawled through air conditioning ducts and overtook the house. The terrorists wanted the president, but he stayed home to watch his favorite nighttime soap opera, so they settled for a stand-off with the government.

The standoff goes on for four months and, over that time, the terrorists and hostages begin to form unlikely friendships. After a few weeks, Roxane decides she must sing in order to maintain her beautiful voice. So, without asking permission from the terrorists, Roxane does so. The terrorists want to make her stop or at the very least control when she sings, but Roxane is not an easy woman to control. And besides, they love to hear her melodic voice as much as everyone else. Her singing eases tensions, calm nerves. Violence or any other kind of ugliness simply cannot exist while she sings.

Hosokawa has been a fan of Roxane for many years and, though they cannot speak the same language, a deep connection develops between them. Using his translator, they learn all they can about one another. Roxane thinks she may love Hosokawa, but she knows that eventually the standoff must end and, when it does, people must die. Roxane, once so anxious to get out, now worries about how it may all end; if she lives, can she really go back to the life she knew before?

What Makes Roxane Coss So Memorable?

Roxane Coss is bold, honorable, and blessed with a rare gift. Even more, she's a woman who has found something wonderful in the midst of a horrific crisis. The manner in which she handles herself while captive is admirable, if not sometimes unwise, and her bold, sassy, American way makes us smile. A character like Roxane Coss doesn't come along often, and for that you won't want to forget her. And when push comes to shove, we can only hope to be a little bit like her.

The Life and Times of Ann Patchett

Born in Los Angeles, but raised in Nashville, Ann Patchett got her first writing break when the *Paris Review* published a story she wrote. She was still attending Sarah Lawrence College at the time. She went on to write for *Seventeen Magazine* for the next nine years.

Patchett wrote her first novel, *Patron Saint of Liars*, while attending the Fine Arts Works Center in Provincetown, Massachusetts. The novel was well liked by readers and critics. Her next two novels were well received, but those books paled in comparison to the huge success of her fourth novel, *Bel Canto*. Patchett was the editor of the 2006 *Best*

American Short Stories anthology and has written for *ELLE*, the *New York Times*, the *Washington Post*, and the *Atlantic*.

FROM *Bel Canto*

A clarification: all of the women were released except one.

She was somewhere in the middle of the line. Like the other women, she was looking back into the living room rather than out the open door, looking back to the floor on which she'd slept like it hadn't been a night but several years. She was looking back at the men who wouldn't be coming outside, none of whom she actually knew. Except the Japanese gentleman whose party this had been, and she certainly didn't *know* him, but he had been helpful with her accompanist, and for that she searched him out and smiled at him. The men shifted from foot to foot in their pack, all of them sad-eyed and nervous from the far side of the room. Mr. Hosokawa returned her smile, a small, dignified acknowledgment, and bowed his head. With the exception of Mr. Hosokawa, the men were not thinking about Roxane Coss then. They had forgotten her and the dizzying heights of her arias. They were watching their wives file out into the bright afternoon, knowing it was a probability that they would never see them again. The love they felt rose up into their throats and blocked the air. There went Edith Thibault, the Vice President's wife, the beautiful Esmeralda.

Roxane Coss was very nearly at the door, perhaps half a dozen women away, when General Hector stepped forward and took her arm. It was not a particularly aggressive gesture. He might have only been trying to escort her someplace, perhaps he had wanted her at the front of the line. "*Espera*," he said, and pointed over to the wall, where she should stand alone near a large Matisse painting of pears and peaches in a bowl. It was one of only two works by Matisse in the entire country and it had been borrowed from the art museum for the party. Roxane, confused, looked at that moment to the translator.

"Wait," Gen said softly in English, trying to make the one word sound as benign as possible. *Wait*, after all, did not mean that she would never go, only that her leaving would be delayed.

Novel Knowledge: THE MANY MEANINGS OF BEL CANTO

Bel canto is Italian for beautiful singing. More specifically, the term refers to a style of singing often heard in eighteenth- and nineteenth-century Italian opera. Bel canto took on a new meaning when, in 1858, Italian composer Rossini used the phrase to describe the lost art of elegant and refined singing in the opera.

She took the word in, thought about it for a moment. She still doubted that's what he had meant even when she heard it in English. As a child she had waited. She had waited at school in line for auditions. But the truth was that in the last several years no one had asked her to wait at all. People waited for her. She did not wait. And all of this, the birthday party, the ridiculous country, the guns, the danger, the *waiting* involved in all of it was a mockery. She pulled her arm back sharply and the jolt caused the General's glasses to slip from his nose. "Look," she said to General Hector, no longer willing to tolerate his hand on her skin. "Enough is enough." Gen opened his mouth to translate and then thought better of it. Besides, she was still speaking. "I came here to do a job, to sing for a party, and I did that. I was told to sleep on the floor with all of these people you have some reason to keep, and I did that, too. But now it's over." She pointed towards the chair where her accompanist sat hunched over. "He's sick. I have to be with him," she said, though it came off as the least convincing of her arguments. Slumped forward in his chair, his arms hanging from his sides like flags on an especially windless day, the accompanist looked more dead than sick. He did not raise his head when she spoke. The line had stopped moving, even the women who were free to go now stopped to watch her, regardless of whether or not they had any idea of what she was saying. It was in this moment of uncertainty, the inevitable pause that comes before the translation, that Roxane Coss saw the moment of her exit. She made a clean move towards the front door, which was open, waiting. General Hector reached up to catch her and, missing her arm, took her firmly by the hair. Such hair made a woman an easy target. It was like being attached to several long soft ropes.

Three things happened in close succession: first, Roxane Coss, lyric soprano, made a clear, high-pitched sound that came from what appeared to be some combination of surprise and actual pain as the tug caused her neck to snap backwards; second, every guest invited to the party (with the exception of her accompanist) stepped forward, making it clear that this was the moment for insurrection; third, every terrorist, ranging from the ages of fourteen to forty-one, cocked the weapon he had been holding and the great metallic click stilled them all like a film spliced into one single frame. And there the room waited, time suspended, until Roxane Coss, without so much as smoothing her dress or touching her hair, turned to go and stand beside a painting that was, in all honesty, a minor work.

After that the Generals began arguing quietly among themselves and even the foot soldiers, the little bandits, were leaning in, trying to hear. Their voices blurred together. The word *woman* was heard and then the words *never* and *agreement*. And then one of them said in a voice that was low and confused, "She could sing." With their heads together there was no telling who said it. It may well have been all of them, all of us.

There were worse reasons to keep a person hostage. You keep someone always for what he or she is worth to you, for what you can trade for her, money or freedom or somebody else you want more. Any person can be a kind of trading chip when you find a way to hold her. So to hold someone for song, because the thing longed for was the sound of her voice, wasn't it all the same? The terrorist, having no chance to get what they came for, decided to take something else instead, something that they never in their lives knew that they wanted until they crouched in the low, dark shaft of the air-conditioning vents: opera. They decided to take that very thing for which Mr. Hosokawa lived.

Roxane waited alone against the wall near the bright, tumbling fruit and cried from frustration. The Generals began to raise their voices while the rest of the women and then the servants filed out. The men glowered and the young terrorists kept their weapons raised. The accompanist, who had momentarily fallen asleep in his chair, roused himself enough to stand and walked out of the room with the help of the kitchen staff, never having realized that his companion was now behind him.

"This is better," General Benjamin said, walking a wide circle on the floor that had previously been covered in hostages. "Now a man can breathe."

From inside they could hear the extraneous hostages being met with great applause and celebration. The bright pop of camera flashes raised up over the other side of the garden wall. In the midst of the confusion, the accompanist walked right back in the front door, which no one had bothered to lock. He threw it open with such force that it slammed back against the wall, the doorknob leaving a mark in the wood. They would have shot him but they knew him. "Roxane Coss is not outside," he said in Swedish. His voice was thick, his consonants catching between his teeth. "She is not outside!"

Novel Knowledge: BOOK AWARDS

Roxane Coss enthralled both readers and critics alike. *Bel Canto* won both the PEN/Faulkner Award and the Orange Prize in 2002, and was a finalist for the National Book Critics Circle Award. It was also named the Book Sense Book of the Year and sold over a million copies in the United States. The book has been translated into thirty languages.

So slurred was the accompanist's speech that it took even Gen a minute to recognize the language. The Swedish he knew was mostly from Bergman films. He had learned it as a college student, matching the subtitles to the sounds. In Swedish, he could only converse on the darkest of subjects. "She's here," Gen said.

The accompanist's health seemed temporarily revived by his fury and for a moment the blood rushed back into his gray cheeks. "All women are released!" He shook his hands in the air as if he were trying to rush crows from a cornfield, his quickly blueing lips were bright with the foam of his spit. Gen relayed the information in Spanish.

"Christopf, here," Roxane said, and gave a small wave as if they had only been briefly separated at a party.

"Take me instead," the accompanist howled, his knees swaying dangerously towards another buckle. It was a delightfully old-fashioned offer, though every person in the room knew that no one wanted him and everyone wanted her.

"Put him outside," General Alfredo said.

Two of the boys stepped forward, but the accompanist, who no one thought was capable of escape in his state of rapid and mysterious deterioration, darted past them and sat down hard on the floor beside Roxane Coss. One of the boys pointed his gun towards the center of his big blond head.

"Don't shoot her accidentally," General Alfredo said.

"What is he saying!" Roxane Coss wailed.

Reluctantly, Gen told her.

Accidentally. That was how people got shot at these things. No real malice, just a bullet a few inches out of place. Roxane Coss cursed every last person in the room as she held her breath. To die because an underskilled terrorist had poor aim was hardly how she had meant to go. The accompanist's breathing was insanely rapid and thin. He closed his eyes and put his head against her leg. His final burst of passion had been enough for him. Just that quickly he was asleep.

"For the sake of God," said General Benjamin, making one of the largest mistakes in a takeover that had been nothing but a series of mistakes, "just leave him there."

As soon as the words were spoken, the accompanist fell forward and vomited up a mouthful of pale yellow foam. Roxane was trying to straighten his legs out again, this time with no one to help her. "At least drag him back outside," she said viciously. "Can't you see there's something wrong with him?" Anyone could see there was something terribly, terribly wrong with him. His skin was wet and cold, the color of the inner flesh of fish gone bad.

Gen put in the request but it was ignored. "No President, one opera singer," General Benjamin said. "It's a rotten exchange if you ask me."

"She's worth more with the piano player," General Alfredo said.

"You couldn't get a dollar for him."

"We keep her," General Hector said quietly, and the subject of opera singers was closed. Though Hector was the least likely to speak, all of the soldiers were most afraid of him. Even the other two Generals exercised caution.

All of the hostages, even Gen, were on the other side of the room from where Roxane and her accompanist were pressed against the wall. Father Arguedas said a prayer quietly and then went to help her. When General Benjamin told him to return to his side of the room he smiled and nodded as if the General was making a little joke and in that sense was not committing a sin. The priest was amazed by the rushing of his heart, by the fear that swept through his legs and made them weak. It was not a fear of being shot, of course, he did not believe they would shoot him, and if they did, well, that would be that. The fear came from the smell of the little bell-shaped lilies and the warm yellow light of her hair. Not since he was fourteen, the year he gave his heart to Christ and put all of those worries behind him, had such things moved him. And why did he feel, in the midst of all this fear and confusion, in the mortal danger of so many lives, the wild giddiness of good luck? What unimaginable good luck! That he had been befriended by Ana Loya, cousin of the Vice President's wife, that she had made such an extravagant request on his behalf, that the request had been graciously granted so that he was allowed to stand in the very back of the room to hear, for the first time in his life, the living opera, and not just sung but sung by Roxane Coss, who was by anyone's account the greatest soprano of our time. That she would have come to such a country to begin with would have been enough. The honor he would have felt lying on his single cot in the basement of the rectory just knowing that she was for one night in the same city in which he lived would have been a miraculous gift. But that he had been allowed to see her and then, by fate (which may well portend awful things, but was still, as was all fate, God's *will*, His wish) he was here now, coming forward to help her with the cumbersome arrangement of her accompanist's gangly limbs, coming close enough to smell the lilies and see her smooth white skin disappearing into the neck of her pistachio-colored gown. He could see that a few of her hairpins remained in place on the crown of her head so that her hair did not fall in her eyes. What a gift, he could not think of it otherwise. Because he believed that such a voice must come from God, then it was God's love he was standing next to now.

And the trembling in his chest, his shaking hands, that was only fitting. How could his heart not be filled with love to be so close to God?

Indiana

IN *INDIANA: A LOVE STORY* BY GEORGE SAND

FIRST PUBLISHED IN: 1832
(TRANSLATED BY GEORGE BURNHAM IVES IN 1900–1902)

Who is she? A high-spirited woman in search of a passionate love who is worthy of her.

Her Story

Indiana is a young Creole woman from Reunion, once called Il Bourbon. While owned by France, the region is an island in the Indian Ocean, and Indiana, like most natives of this region, grew up isolated from the rest of France. She married Colonel Delmare, a man old enough to be her father, in order to escape her own abusive father. While she never loved the Colonel he seemed, at the time, like the best way out of a bad situation—a decision she rethinks over the course of the novel.

There are two other men in Indiana's life—her melancholy cousin, Ralph, and a handsome playboy named Raymon. Both underestimate Indiana. When Raymon takes an interest in her, she falls in love—for the first time in her life. She can't stop thinking about him, even after the Colonel moves them back to Il Bourbon. In fact, one night Indiana escapes the house and goes to Raymon thinking that the two are meant to be together, but as he tries to seduce her, she is resistant. Raymon is surprised and perturbed to know that the will of this young, naive woman is so strong that she can resist him. From that moment on, his efforts to make her fall in love with him are purely to prove he can. He doesn't love her. She understands this but wants to call his bluff. And she will stop at nothing to see that she does.

Still, Indiana is lonely and heartbroken that Raymon—or, she feels, any other man—will never love her. But Indiana hasn't considered the feelings of her cousin Ralph. When the two finally find a quiet moment alone together, they admit to themselves and to each other their true feelings. Through their confessions, they find a lot of answers, love, and ultimately happiness they hadn't known with each other lovers.

What Makes Indiana So Memorable?

Indiana is a small woman with a bold soul, a boundless zest for life, and limitless energy for love. She is romantic and high-spirited. She astonishes people when she fox hunts with as much speed and tenacity as any man. She brings down men's egos when they find they cannot seduce her easily, and there is a surprising sting to the letters she writes.

Everyone who knows Indiana underestimates her. She is a force to be reckoned with, but it seems to be hard for others to give her credit. It is easier for people to believe that the best qualities and actions of this small-framed Creole girl are simply flukes, rather than signs of a strong woman. This does not bother Indiana, however. She simply plays the games that people want to play and she makes the most of each situation she finds herself in.

The Life and Times of George Sand (Amantine Aurore Lucile Dupin)

Amantine Aurore Lucile Dupin, later Baroness Dudevant, is best known under the pen name of George Sand.

Sand was born in 1804 and was raised by her grandmother after her mother moved to Paris to start a new life. When her grandmother died in 1821, she was in a rush to marry. So, in 1822, much like her character

Indiana, she married Casimir Dudevant, a much older man whom she didn't really love. Together, they had two children, Maurice and Solange. In 1836, after fourteen years of marriage, she left Dudevant. Two years later, she fell in love with Jules Sandeau and together they wrote and published a novel titled *Rose et Blanche* under the name J. Sand. When an editor wanted to publish *Indiana: A Love Story* under the same pen name, Jules didn't think it would be right for him to accept credit for a work he didn't write. They agreed to change the first name but leave the last, and so George Sand was created.

Soon after the success of *Indiana*, Sand wrote her second novel, *Valentine*, which proved equally as popular. Her third novel, *Lélia*, cemented her as a famous writer in France. In fact, she found herself at the center of France's finest literary circle and was as well paid as Honoré de Balzac and Victor Hugo. Her personal life and outspoken political views also kept her in the limelight. She was a staunch supporter of equal rights for all men and women and she was known to have affairs with both sexes. She was always searching for a great love. She had this to say about the subject: "Don't walk in front of me, I may not follow. Don't walk behind me, I may not lead. There is only one happiness in life, to love and be loved." Whether or not she found love is hard to know. After her first marriage, she had no interest in marrying again, only loving and being loved. She died in June of 1876 in Nohant, near Châteauroux. She was seventy-one years old.

From *Indiana: A Love Story*

Raymon was amazed at what seemed to take place in Indiana's being as soon as the hounds were away. Her eyes gleamed, her cheeks flushed, the dilation of her nostrils betrayed an indefinable thrill of fear or pleasure, and suddenly, driving her spurs into her horse's side, she left him and galloped after Ralph. Raymon did not know that hunting was the only passion that Ralph and Indiana had in common. Nor did he suspect that in that frail and apparently timid woman there abode a more than masculine courage, that sort of delirious intrepidity which sometimes manifests itself like a nervous paroxysm in the feeblest creatures. Women rarely have the physical courage which consists in offering the resistance of inertia to pain or danger; but they often have the moral courage which attains its climax in peril or suffering. Indiana's delicate fibres delighted above all things in the tumult, the rapid movement and the excitement of the chase, that miniature image of war with its fatigues, its stratagems, its calculations, its hazards and its battles. Her dull, ennui-laden life needed this excitement; at such times she seemed to wake from a lethargy and to expend in one day all the energy that she had left to ferment uselessly in her blood for a whole year.

Raymon was terrified to see her ride away so fast, abandoning herself fearlessly to the impetuous spirit of a horse that she hardly knew, rushing him through the thickets, avoiding with amazing skill the branches that lashed at her face as they sprang back, leaping ditches without hesitation, venturing confidently on clayey, slippery ground, heedless of the risk of breaking her slender limbs, but eager to be first on the smoking scent of the boar. So much determination alarmed him and nearly disgusted him with Madame Delmare. Men, especially lovers, are addicted to the innocent fatuity of preferring to protect weakness rather than to admire courage in womankind. Shall I confess it? Raymon was terrified at the promise of high spirit and tenacity in love which such intrepidity seemed to afford. It was not like the resignation of poor Noun, who preferred to drown herself rather than to contend against her misfortunes.

"If there's as much vigor and excitement in her tenderness as there is in her diversions," he thought; "if her will clings to me, fierce and palpitating, as her caprice clings to that boar's quarters, why society will impose no fetters on her, the law will have no force; my destiny will have to succumb and I shall have to sacrifice my future to her present."

Novel Knowledge: AFFAIRS TO REMEMBER

When Sand was thirty-three she began an affair with the famous composer Chopin. At first Chopin didn't find her attractive. He was quoted as saying "Something about her repels me," but he clearly changed his mind. Sand and Chopin's relationship ended abruptly in 1847 when Sand began to suspect that Chopin was having an affair with her daughter, Solange. She was right. Chopin had indeed fallen in love with Solange.

Cries of terror and distress, among which he could distinguish Madame Delmare's voice, roused Raymon from these reflections. He anxiously urged his horse forward and was soon overtaken by Ralph, who asked him if he had heard the outcries.

At that moment several terrified whippers-in rode up to them, crying out confusedly that the boar had charged and overthrown Madame Delmare. Other huntsmen, in still greater dismay, appeared, calling for Sir Ralph, whose surgical skill was required by the injured person.

"It's of no use," said a late arrival. "There is no hope, your help will be too late."

In that moment of horror, Raymon's eyes fell upon the pale, gloomy features of Monsieur Brown. He did not cry out, he did not foam at the mouth, he did not wring his hands; he simply took out his hunting-knife and with a *sang-froid* truly English was preparing to cut his own throat, when Raymon snatched the weapon from him and hurried him in the direction from which the cries came.

Ralph felt as if he were waking from a dream when he saw Madame Delmare rush to meet him and urge him forward to the assistance of her husband, who lay on the ground, apparently lifeless. Sir Ralph made haste to bleed him; for he had speedily satisfied himself that he was not dead; but his leg was broken and he was taken to the château.

As for Madame Delmare, in the confusion her name had been substituted by accident for that of her husband, or perhaps Ralph and Raymon had erroneously thought that they heard the name in which they were most interested.

Novel Knowledge: Head-Turning Fashion

Sand wore men's clothing in public claiming that they were more durable, comfortable, and less expensive than women's clothing. This, along with her tobacco- and cigar-smoking, caused quite a stir in Paris.

Indiana was uninjured, but her fright and consternation had almost taken away her power of locomotion. Raymon supported her in his arms and was reconciled to her womanly heart when he saw how deeply affected she was by the misfortune of a husband whom she had much to forgive before pitying him.

Sir Ralph had already recovered his accustomed tranquillity; but an extraordinary pallor revealed the violent shock he had experienced; he had nearly lost one of the two human beings whom he loved.

Raymon, who alone, in that moment of confusion and excitement, had retained sufficient presence of mind to understand what he saw, had been able to judge of Ralph's affection for his cousin, and how little it was balanced by his feeling for the colonel. This observation, which positively contradicted Indiana's opinion, did not depart from Raymon's memory as it did from that of the other witnesses of the scene.

However Raymon never mentioned to Madame Delmare the attempted suicide of which he had been a witness. In this ungenerous reserve there was a suggestion of selfishness and bad temper which you will forgive perhaps in view of the amorous jealousy which was responsible for it.

After six weeks the colonel was with much difficulty removed to Lagny; but it was more than six months thereafter before he could walk; for before the fractured femur was fairly reduced he had an acute attack of rheumatism in the injured leg, which condemned him to excruciating pain and absolute immobility. His wife lavished the most loving attentions upon him; she never left his bedside and endured without a complaint his bitter fault-finding humor, his soldier-like testiness and his invalid's injustice.

Despite the ennui of such a depressing life, her health became robust and flourishing once more and happiness took up its abode in her heart. Raymon loved her, he really loved her. He came every day; he was discouraged by no difficulty in the way of seeing her, he bore with the infirmities of her husband, her cousin's coldness, the constraint of their interviews. A glance from him filled Indiana's heart with joy for a whole day. She no longer thought of complaining of life; her heart was full, her youthful nature had ample employment, her moral force had something to feed upon.

The colonel gradually came to feel very friendly to Raymon. He was simple enough to believe that his neighbor's assiduity in calling upon him was a proof of the interest he took in his health. Madame de Ramière also came occasionally, to sanction the liaison by her presence, and Indiana became warmly and passionately attached to Raymon's mother. At last the wife's lover became the husband's friend.

Winnie Louie

IN *THE KITCHEN GOD'S WIFE* BY AMY TAN
FIRST PUBLISHED IN: 1991

Who is she? A remarkably stubborn and resilient woman who starts a new life in a new world.

Her Story

Winnie Louie has not led an easy life. But after years of keeping so much of her dark past a secret, Winnie decides to tell her American-born daughter about the hardships and horrors she endured as a girl in China.

In vivid detail, Winnie recalls her life as a child after her own mother abandoned her, and as a young bride attempting to please her first husband, Wen Fu. She recalls the day she defied Wen Fu and how her defiance led to more abuse. She remembers the bloodshed from the Japanese war on China as though it happened yesterday. Yet, the secrets she has kept from her daughter all these years are not all ugly. She talks about the night she met Jimmie Louie, the Chinese-American translator. And how, after that night, with a glimpse of hope, and the help of friends, Winnie managed to escape China. By revealing her past, Winnie draws her daughter closer to her—hoping, perhaps, that her daughter will share secrets too.

What Makes Winnie Louie So Memorable?

Winnie Louie is remarkably stubborn, and this trait can be a detriment or an asset depending on the situation. For Winnie, however, the situation didn't matter. She did what she felt was honest and right no matter the benefit—or the consequence. When Wen Fu wanted her to say she liked his favorite meal, she wouldn't do it. Night after night, he instructed the servants to prepare his favorite dish hoping that she would give in and say she liked it. She never did. She ate it and she didn't complain, but she never gave Wen Fu the satisfaction; he eventually gave up.

To lie about her feelings, even about little things, for the sake of getting along with the man she was forced to marry is unacceptable in Winnie's mind. This is even more remarkable when you consider the fact that, in Winnie's world of Chinese Confucian ideals, a woman isn't even supposed to express her opinions. Winnie counteracts this ideal time and time again.

"But if I didn't fight, would that be like admitting my life was finished?"

Equally as remarkable is Winnie's resilience. Despite the abuse of Wen Fu, and the Japanese invasion of China, her heart does not harden. She still believes in love. She still has hope. And perhaps most striking of all, she has the courage and the will to start over.

The Life and Times of Amy Tan

Born in 1952, in California, Amy Tan is a first generation Chinese American. Her books explore the relationships between women—often between mothers and daughters—who are struggling with cultural and generational divides. Her first novel, *The Joy Luck Club*, was a bestseller. She has also written two children's books. One, *The Chinese Siamese Cat*, was made into an animated series on PBS. Tired of reading a lot of things about her own life that simply weren't true, Tan started her own website *www.amytan.net* to clear up ridiculous rumors and silly lies. For example, Tan has not won the Nobel Prize for Literature—she clears up this point on her site. She has been nominated and won a number of other prestigious awards, so perhaps someday she will earn the Nobel, too. Tan currently lives in the San Francisco area.

FROM *The Kitchen God's Wife*

By the time I left Peanut's place, it was already late in the afternoon. I had to hurry to the bookshop to find your father. The whole way there I was smiling big, I could not stop myself. And it seemed to me other people on the road saw my happiness and smiled back to congratulate me.

As soon as I saw your father, I told him: "In a week or two, I am leaving my marriage." I was trembling, both proud and nervous.

"Is this really so?" he said. He was trembling too.

Novel Knowledge: CRITICS LOVE IT

The Kitchen God's Wife earned the *Booklist* Editor's Choice Award, an American Library Association Notable Book Award, and a spot on the *New York Times* Notable Book list.

"Really so," I said. He held my hands, and we were laughing with tears in our eyes.

If your father were still alive today, I think he would agree. We knew then we would always be together. I do not know how two strangers knew this, how we could be so sure. But maybe it was like this: When he put that photo of four daughters on the table, that was like asking me to marry him. And when I ran back and said I was leaving my marriage, that was like saying I accepted.

And from that moment on, we were together, two people talking with one heart.

"And next?" he was asking me. "What must we do next?"

"We must wait awhile," I said. "We must wait until the right moment when I can leave."

And then we made a plan. When I was ready to run away, I would call him by telephone late at night when everybody was sleeping. I would say something very quick and simple, such as, "Tomorrow I'm coming."

But then your father, he was so romantic, he suggested something else, a secret code. So this is what we decided I would say: "Open the door, you can already see the mountain," which is a classical saying, meaning you're ready to grab all opportunities and turn them into something big. Your father would answer me this way: "Let's go beyond the mountain." And then he would meet me and Danru the next day at the harbor, in front of the booth that sold tickets to Tsungming Island. And there we would get into a car that would take us to Peanut's place.

When I returned home that day, I saw my life as if I already knew the happy ending of a story. I looked around the house and thought, Soon I will no longer have to see these walls and all the unhappiness they keep inside.

I heard Wen Fu's mother shouting at the cook, and I imagined myself eating a simple, quiet meal without having my stomach turn itself inside out. I saw Wen Fu walk in the door, and I thought, Soon I will no longer have to rub my skin off, trying to remove his stain from my body. I saw Danru watching his father out of the corner of his eye, and I thought, Soon my son can laugh and play without any fears.

And then I saw my father, his back bent, shuffling into his study. It seemed as if I had never seen my father look so weak.

And that's when I remembered, My father! If I leave, Wen Fu will have him killed as a traitor. He would use my father just like a weapon.

I quickly went upstairs to my room. I began to argue with myself. I should let my father go to prison, I thought. After all, he brought this on himself. Let him see what it is like to suffer.

And then I thought of more reasons. He was the one who mistreated my own mother! He was the one who refused to see me when I was growing up. He was the one who let me marry a bad man. He did not care that he was giving me an unhappy future. Why should I sacrifice my happiness for him? There had never been love between us, father to daughter, daughter to father.

But all those angry reasons only made me feel I was as evil as Wen Fu. So I emptied those feelings from my heart. I quietly excused myself: He is old. His mind is already gone. How can I be responsible for what Wen Fu does to him?

And still I knew: Those excuses would not cover anything up, the real reason. So in the end, all the excuses fell away, and I saw only one thing: Jimmy Louie.

I no longer denied I was betraying my father. I no longer looked for excuses. I knew what I was doing was both true and wrong. I could not make just one choice, I had to make two: Let me live. Let my father die.

Isn't that how it is when you must decide with your heart? You are not just choosing one thing over another. You are choosing what you want. And you are also choosing what somebody else does not want, and all the consequences that follow. You can tell yourself, That's not my problem, but those words do not wash the trouble away. Maybe it is no longer a problem in your life. But it is always a problem in your heart. And I can tell you, that afternoon, when I knew what I wanted, I cried, just like a child who cannot explain why she is crying.

The next week I was a person in mourning. I felt I had already lost my father, also a part of myself. I wanted to be comforted. I wanted to be miserable. And then one afternoon, without thinking, I found myself following my father into his study. I don't know why, maybe I wanted to let him know in some way that I was sorry.

"Father," I called to him. He looked up at me, without expression. I sat down in a chair opposite him. "Father," I said again. "Do you know who I am?"

This time he did not look at me. He was staring at the wall, at the same ancient scroll painting he had ruined with a cup of tea that afternoon the Japanese came.

The painting showed the springtime, pink flowers blossoming on trees, the trees growing on a mountain, the mountain rising up out of a misty lake. At the bottom was a black lacquer rod, weighing it down. You could tell the scroll had once been part of a set, the four seasons. But now the three other seasons were gone, sold by Wen Fu, and only their empty spots hung on the wall, like ghost paintings. And you could also tell why this scroll had been left behind—the big tea stain at the center, as if the painted lake had flooded itself.

"Isn't it strange," I said to my father, "that someone would want only three seasons? Like a life that will never be completed."

Of course, my father did not answer. And because I thought my father could not understand anything, I continued to talk non-sense. "My life has been like that painting nobody wants, the same season, every day the same misery, no hope of changing."

And now I was crying. "That's why I must find a way to leave my marriage. I do not expect you to forgive me."

My father sat up straight. He stared at me with one sad eye, one angry eye. I was startled to see this, that he had heard what I said. He stood up. His mouth moved up and down. But no words would come out, he could only chew the air with "uh! uh!" sounds. A terrible expression grew on his face. He waved his hands in front of his face, as if the words stuck in his throat were choking him.

My father reached out with one shaky hand. He grabbed my arm, and I was surprised how strong he still was. He was pulling me out of my chair, toward the scroll. "I must," I whispered to him. "You don't know how much I have suffered." He waved my words away.

And then he let go of my arm. His two trembly hands were now fighting with the black lacquer rod. I thought he wanted to pick up that rod and strike me over the head. But instead, he suddenly pulled the knob off the rod, and out poured three little gold ingots into his waiting palm.

He pressed them into my hand, then stared at me. I was struggling so hard to know his meaning. And I can still see the two expressions on his face when I finally understood. One side was agony, the other relief, as if he wanted to say to me, "You foolish, foolish girl, finally you've made the right decision."

"I cannot take them now," I whispered. "Wen Fu would find them. Later I will get them, right before I leave." My father nodded once, then quickly put the gold ingots back into their hiding place.

I have thought about this many times. I do not think my father was saying he loved me. I think he was telling me that if I left this terrible man, then maybe this terrible man would leave his house too. Maybe my father and his wives would no longer have to suffer. My leaving was their only chance. Of course, maybe he was telling me he loved me a little, too.

The next morning was very strange for me. Everyone came downstairs for the morning meal: Wen Fu, Danru, Wen Fu's mother and father, San Ma and Wu Ma. The servant brought in a bowl of steaming soup.

If you had been there, you would think nothing had changed. My father did not seem to recognize me. Once again, his mind seemed as cloudy as the soup he stared at. Wen Fu's mother had only complaints: The soup was not hot enough, the soup was too salty. Wen Fu ate without speaking. I wondered if I had dreamt what happened the day before, if I had only imagined the gold ingots. I was nervous, but I vowed to go ahead with my plans, what I had decided the night before.

I poured Wen Fu's mother more soup. "Mother," I said to her, "eat more, take care of your health." As she drank, I continued my conversation. "Poor Old Aunt. Her health is not so good. I had a letter from her yesterday."

This was true. I had received a letter, and as usual, Old Aunt complained about her health. She could be counted on for that.

"What's the matter with her?" asked Wu Ma. She worried a lot about her own health.

"A coldness in her bones, a lack of force at the end of each breath. She feels she might die any day."

"That old woman never feels well," said Wen Fu's mother in an unkind voice. "She has an ailment to match every herb grown on the earth."

Wen Fu laughed in agreement.

"This time I really think she is sick," I said. And then I added in a quiet voice, "Her color was very bad the last time I saw her. No heat. Now she says she is worse."

"Perhaps you better go see her," said San Ma.

"Mmmm," I murmured, as if I had not considered this before. "Perhaps you are right."

"The girl just got back!" exclaimed Wen Fu's mother.

"Maybe I could go for a short visit. If she is not too sick, I'll come home in a day or two."

And Wen Fu's mother only said, "Hnnh!"

"Of course, if she is really sick, I may have to stay longer."

But now the cook had brought in the steamed dumplings, and Wen Fu's mother was too busy inspecting and criticizing the food to give me any more trouble.

So you see, she did not say yes, but she did not say no, either. I knew then that if I left the next day holding a suitcase with one hand and Danru with the other, nobody would think anything of it. And if I did not return home after three or four days, no one would go looking for me. They would only say, "Poor Old Aunt, sicker than we thought."

That afternoon, while everyone slept, I walked quickly into my father's study and shut the door. I went over to the scroll of spring-time. I shook the rod. Sure enough, the weight of those three ingots slid back and forth. Then bright gold fell into my hand. And I saw that what had happened the day before was true, not my imagination.

Anna Arkadyevna Karenina

IN *ANNA KARENINA* BY LEO TOLSTOY
FIRST PUBLISHED IN: 1873–1877
(TRANSLATED BY CONSTANCE GARNETT IN 1901)

Who is she? A woman obsessed with what she cannot have.

Her Story

When Anna Karenina meets Count Vronsky, she is certain she has found her one true love. Fortunately, her husband doesn't mind. As far as he's concerned, Anna can love whomever she wants as long as she doesn't create gossip. But Anna doesn't hold up her end of the bargain. She even becomes a public embarrassment to her husband when she overacts to a race horse accident involving Vronsky. Soon, her affair with the Count has all of Moscow's high society judging her harshly.

Eventually, Anna leaves her husband and her children in order to start a new life with the Count. But no matter where the two go, society overlooks Vronsky's indiscretions, but not Anna's. While Vronksy is invited to social galas and intimate parties, Anna is not. Soon, Vronsky begins to accept these invitations, leaving Anna at home alone, and their romance begins to unravel. Since life is the same no matter where the couple go, they decide they may as well return to Moscow. Anna has made a mess of her life and she knows it. She cries for help. Unfortunately, no one wants to listen to her anymore.

What Makes Anna Arkadyevna Karenina So Memorable?

Clearly, Tolstoy set out to create an unforgettable woman. First, he names the book after her despite a number of other major characters. Then, he uses a portrait of Anna to describe her before the reader ever meets her, which causes her to take on a larger-than-life, Mona Lisa–esque quality, "It was not a picture, but a living, charming woman, with black curling hair, with bare arms and shoulders, with a pensive smile on the lips, covered with soft down; triumphantly and softly she looked at him with eyes that baffled him. She was not living only because she was more beautiful than a living woman can be."

Anna is not admirable, nor is she strong or resolute. She is simply a beautiful woman who continuously makes the wrong decision and pays dearly for always wanting things that are out of her control. Like her beauty, her story is hard to forget. She is a victim of high society Moscow where people are not easily forgiven for their mistakes and looking down on others is a favorite pastime.

The Life and Times of Leo Tolstoy

Count Leo Nikolayevich Tolstoy was born into Russian nobility in 1828. His parents both died when he was still a boy so his relatives raised him. He studied law and languages, but did not have the temperament for university life so he quit and moved to Moscow where he took to gambling and racked up debts. Eventually, he settled down with Sophie, a woman sixteen years younger than him. Together, they had thirteen children. During the early years of their marriage, Tolstoy found the support and tranquility he needed to write *War and Peace* and *Anna Karenina*. Later, however, as his political and spiritual views became more unconventional, even radical, he and his wife began to fight. When he refused his inheritance and his writing royalties as a statement of his views, his marriage completely fell apart. He left Sophie in 1910, when he was eighty-two years old. He wandered in the harsh Russian winter for ten days and died at the Astopov Station, presumably of pneumonia.

FROM *Anna Karenina*

When Alexey Alexandrovitch reached the race-course, Anna was already sitting in the pavilion beside Betsy, in that pavilion where all the highest society had gathered. She caught sight of her husband in the distance. Two men, her husband and her lover, were the two centers of her existence, and unaided by her external senses she was aware of their nearness. She was aware of her husband approaching a long way off, and she could not help following him in the surging crowd in the midst of which he was moving. She watched his progress towards the pavilion, saw him now responding condescendingly to an ingratiating bow, now exchanging friendly, nonchalant greetings with his equals, now assiduously trying to catch the eye of some great one of this world, and taking off his big round hat that squeezed the tips of his ears. All these ways of his she knew, and all were hateful to her. "Nothing but ambition, nothing but the desire to get on, that's all there is in his soul," she thought; "as for these lofty ideals, love of culture, religion, they are only so many tools for getting on."

From his glances towards the ladies' pavilion (he was staring straight at her, but did not distinguish his wife in the sea of muslin, ribbons, feathers, parasols and flowers) she saw that he was looking for her, but she purposely avoided noticing him.

"Alexey Alexandrovitch!" Princess Betsy called to him; "I'm sure you don't see your wife: here she is."

He smiled his chilly smile.

"There's so much splendor here that one's eyes are dazzled," he said, and he went into the pavilion. He smiled to his wife as a man should smile on meeting his wife after only just parting from her, and greeted the princess and other acquaintances, giving to each what was due—that is to say, jesting with the ladies and dealing out friendly greetings among the men. Below, near the pavilion, was standing an adjutant-general of whom Alexey Alexandrovitch had a high opinion, noted for his intelligence and culture. Alexey Alexandrovitch entered into conversation with him.

There was an interval between the races, and so nothing hindered conversation. The adjutant-general expressed his disapproval of races. Alexey Alexandrovitch replied defending them. Anna heard his high, measured tones, not losing one word, and every word struck her as false, and stabbed her ears with pain.

Novel Knowledge: THE WOMAN BEHIND *ANNA KARENINA*

The character of Anna Karenina was likely inspired by Maria Hartung, the eldest daughter of the great Russian poet Alexander Pushkin. Tolstoy met her at a dinner one evening and began reading Pushkin and daydreaming about the young lady who made an impression on him.

When the three-mile steeplechase was beginning, she bent forward and gazed with fixed eyes at Vronsky as he went up to his horse and mounted, and at the same time she heard that loathsome, never-ceasing voice of her husband. She was in an agony of terror for Vronsky, but a still greater agony was the never-ceasing, as it seemed to her, stream of her husband's shrill voice with its familiar intonations.

"I'm a wicked woman, a lost woman," she thought; "but I don't like lying, I can't endure falsehood, while as for him (her husband) it's the breath of his life—falsehood. He knows all about it, he sees it all; what does he care if he can talk so calmly? If he were to kill me, if he were to kill Vronsky, I might respect him. No, all he wants is falsehood and propriety," Anna said to herself, not considering exactly what it was she wanted of her husband, and how she would have liked to see him behave. She did not understand either that Alexey Alexandrovitch's peculiar loquacity that day, so exasperating to her, was merely the expression of his inward distress and uneasiness. As a child that has been hurt skips about, putting all his muscles into movement to drown the pain, in the same way Alexey Alexandrovitch needed mental exercise to drown the thoughts of his wife that in her presence and in Vronsky's, and with the continual iteration of his name, would force themselves on his attention. And it was as natural for him to talk well and cleverly, as it is natural for a child to skip about. He was saying:

"Danger in the races of officers, of cavalry men, is an essential element in the race. If England can point to the most brilliant feats of cavalry in military history, it is simply owing to the fact that she has historically developed this force both in beasts and in men. Sport has, in my opinion, a great value, and as is always the case, we see nothing but what is most superficial."

"It's not superficial," said Princess Tverskaya. "One of the officers, they say, has broken two ribs."

Alexey Alexandrovitch smiled his smile, which uncovered his teeth, but revealed nothing more.

"We'll admit, princess, that that's not superficial," he said, "but internal. But that's not the point," and he turned again to the general with whom he was talking seriously; "we mustn't forget that those who are taking part in the race are military men, who have chosen that career, and one must allow that every calling has its disagreeable side. It forms an integral part of the duties of an officer. Low sports, such as prize-fighting or Spanish bull-fights, are a sign of barbarity. But specialized trials of skill are a sign of development."

"No, I shan't come another time; it's too upsetting," said Princess Betsy. "Isn't it, Anna?"

"It is upsetting, but one can't tear oneself away," said another lady. "If I'd been a Roman woman I should never have missed a single circus."

Anna said nothing, and keeping her opera glass up, gazed always at the same spot.

At that moment a tall general walked through the pavilion. Breaking off what he was saying, Alexey Alexandrovitch got up hurriedly, though with dignity, and bowed low to the general.

"You're not racing?" the officer asked, chaffing him.

"My race is a harder one," Alexey Alexandrovitch responded deferentially.

And though the answer meant nothing, the general looked as though he had heard a witty remark from a witty man, and fully relished *la pointe de la sauce*.

"There are two aspects," Alexey Alexandrovitch resumed: "those who take part and those who look on; and love for such spectacles is an unmistakable proof of a low degree of development in the spectator, I admit, but . . ."

"Princess, bets!" sounded Stepan Arkadyevitch's voice from below, addressing Betsy. "Who's your favorite?"

"Anna and I are for Kuzovlev," replied Betsy.

"I'm for Vronsky. A pair of gloves?"

"Done!"

"But it is a pretty sight, isn't it?"

Alexey Alexandrovitch paused while there was talking about him, but he began again directly.

"I admit that manly sports do not . . ." he was continuing.

But at that moment the racers started, and all conversation ceased. Alexey Alexandrovitch too was silent, and everyone stood up and turned towards the stream. Alexey Alexandrovitch took no interest in the race, and so he did not watch the racers, but fell listlessly to scanning the spectators with his weary eyes. His eyes rested upon Anna.

Her face was white and set. She was obviously seeing nothing and no one but one man. Her hand had convulsively clutched her fan, and she held her breath. He looked at her and hastily turned away, scrutinizing other faces.

"But here's this lady too, and others very much moved as well; it's very natural," Alexey Alexandrovitch told himself. He tried not to look at her, but unconsciously his eyes were drawn to her.

He examined that face again, trying not to read what was so plainly written on it, and against his own will, with horror read on it what he did not want to know.

The first fall—Kuzovlev's, at the stream—agitated everyone, but Alexey Alexandrovitch saw distinctly on Anna's pale, triumphant face that the man she was watching had not fallen. When, after Mahotin and Vronsky had cleared the worst barrier, the next officer had been thrown straight on his head at it and fatally injured, and a shudder of horror passed over the whole public, Alexey Alexandrovitch saw that Anna did not even notice it, and had some difficulty in realizing what they were talking of about her. But more and more often, and with greater persistence, he watched her. Anna, wholly engrossed as she was with the race, became aware of her husband's cold eyes fixed upon her from one side.

She glanced round for an instant, looked inquiringly at him, and with a slight frown turned away again.

"Ah, I don't care!" she seemed to say to him, and she did not once glance at him again.

The race was an unlucky one, and of the seventeen officers who rode in it more than half were thrown and hurt. Towards the end of the race everyone was in a state of agitation, which was intensified by the fact that the Tsar was displeased.

* * *

Everyone was loudly expressing disapprobation, everyone was repeating a phrase some one had uttered—"The lions and gladiators will be the next thing," and everyone was feeling horrified; so that when Vronsky fell to the ground, and Anna moaned aloud, there was nothing very out of the way in it. But afterwards a change came over Anna's face which really was beyond decorum. She utterly lost her head. She began fluttering like a caged bird, at one moment would have got up and moved away, at the next turned to Betsy.

"Let us go, let us go!" she said.

But Betsy did not hear her. She was bending down, talking to a general who had come up to her.

Alexey Alexandrovitch went up to Anna and courteously offered her his arm.

"Let us go, if you like," he said in French, but Anna was listening to the general and did not notice her husband.

"He's broken his leg too, so they say," the general was saying. "This is beyond everything."

Without answering her husband, Anna lifted her opera glass and gazed towards the place where Vronsky had fallen; but it was so far off, and there was such a crowd of people about it, that she could make out nothing. She laid down the opera glass, and would have moved away, but at that moment an officer galloped up and made some announcement to the Tsar. Anna craned forward listening.

"Stiva! Stiva!" she cried to her brother.

But her brother did not hear her. Again she would have moved away.

"Once more I offer you my arm if you want to be going," said Alexey Alexandrovitch, reaching towards her hand.

She drew back from him with aversion, and without looking in his face answered:

"No, no, let me be, I'll stay."

She saw now that from the place of Vronsky's accident an officer was running across the course towards the pavilion. Betsy waved her handkerchief to him. The officer brought the news that the rider was not killed, but the horse had broken its back.

On hearing this Anna sat down hurriedly, and hid her face in her fan. Alexey Alexandrovitch saw that she was weeping, and could not control her tears, nor even the sobs that were shaking her bosom. Alexey Alexandrovitch stood so as to screen her, giving her time to recover herself.

"For the third time I offer you my arm," he said to her after a little time, turning to her. Anna gazed at him and did not know what to say. Princess Betsy came to her rescue.

"No, Alexey Alexandrovitch; I brought Anna and I promised to take her home," put in Betsy.

"Excuse me, princess," he said, smiling courteously but looking her very firmly in the face, "but I see that Anna's not very well, and I wish her to come home with me."

Anna looked about her in a frightened way, got up submissively, and laid her hand on her husband's arm.

"I'll send to him and find out, and let you know," Betsy whispered to her.

As they left the pavilion, Alexey Alexandrovitch, as always, talked to those he met, and Anna had, as always, to talk and answer; but she was utterly beside herself, and moved hanging on her husband's arm as though in a dream.

"Is he killed or not? Is it true? Will he come or not? Shall I see him today?" she was thinking.

She took her seat in her husband's carriage in silence, and in silence drove out of the crowd of carriages. In spite of all he had seen, Alexey Alexandrovitch still did not allow himself to consider his wife's real condition. He merely saw the outward symptoms. He saw that she was behaving unbecomingly, and considered it his duty to tell her so. But it was very difficult for him not to say more, to tell her nothing but that. He opened his mouth to tell her she had behaved unbecomingly, but he could not help saying something utterly different.

"What an inclination we all have, though, for these cruel spectacles," he said. "I observe . . ."

"Eh? I don't understand," said Anna contemptuously.

He was offended, and at once began to say what he had meant to say.

"I am obliged to tell you," he began.

"So now we are to have it out," she thought, and she felt frightened.

"I am obliged to tell you that your behavior has been unbecoming today," he said to her in French.

"In what way has my behavior been unbecoming?" she said aloud, turning her head swiftly and looking him straight in the face, not with the bright expression that seemed covering something, but with a look of determination, under which she concealed with difficulty the dismay she was feeling.

"Mind," he said, pointing to the open window opposite the coachman.

He got up and pulled up the window.

"What did you consider unbecoming?" she repeated.

"The despair you were unable to conceal at the accident to one of the riders."

He waited for her to answer, but she was silent, looking straight before her.

"I have already begged you so to conduct yourself in society that even malicious tongues can find nothing to say against you. There was a time when I spoke of your inward attitude, but I am not speaking of that now. Now I speak only of your external attitude. You have behaved improperly, and I would wish it not to occur again."

She did not hear half of what he was saying; she felt panic-stricken before him, and was thinking whether it was true that Vronsky was not killed. Was it of him they were speaking when they said the rider was unhurt, but the horse had broken its back? She merely smiled with a pretense of irony when he finished, and made no reply, because she had not heard what he said. Alexey Alexandrovitch had begun to speak boldly, but as he realized plainly what he was speaking of, the dismay she was feeling infected him too. He saw the smile, and a strange misapprehension came over him.

"She is smiling at my suspicions. Yes, she will tell me directly what she told me before; that there is no foundation for my suspicions, that it's absurd."

At that moment, when the revelation of everything was hanging over him, there was nothing he expected so much as that she would answer mockingly as before that his suspicions were absurd and utterly groundless. So terrible to him was what he knew that now he was ready to believe anything. But the expression of her face, scared and gloomy, did not now promise even deception.

Novel Knowledge: A BESTSELLER 100 YEARS LATER

In 2004, Oprah Winfrey recommended *Anna Karenina* for her book club, thereby making the novel an American bestseller over 100 years after its original publication.

"Possibly I was mistaken," said he. "If so, I beg your pardon."

"No, you were not mistaken," she said deliberately, looking desperately into his cold face. "You were not mistaken. I was, and I could not help being in despair. I hear you, but I am thinking of him. I love him, I am his mistress; I can't bear you; I'm afraid of you, and I hate you. . . . You can do what you like to me."

And dropping back into the corner of the carriage, she broke into sobs, hiding her face in her hands. Alexey Alexandrovitch did not stir, and kept looking straight before him. But his whole face suddenly bore the solemn rigidity of the dead, and his expression did not change during the whole time of the drive home. On reaching the house he turned his head to her, still with the same expression.

"Very well! But I expect a strict observance of the external forms of propriety till such time"—his voice shook—"as I may take measures to secure my honor and communicate them to you."

He got out first and helped her to get out. Before the servants he pressed her hand, took his seat in the carriage, and drove back to Petersburg. Immediately afterwards a footman came from Princess Betsy and brought Anna a note.

Countess Ellen Mingott Olenska

IN *THE AGE OF INNOCENCE* BY EDITH WHARTON

FIRST PUBLISHED IN: 1920

Who is she? An elusive, free-spirited woman in a world where everyone is supposed to conform.

Her Story

Countess Ellen Olenska is done turning a blind eye to her husband's infidelities. After years abroad, she returns to New York to get a quick divorce from the Polish Count and, in her words, "cast off all my old life, to become just like everybody else here." She learns that there is little chance of a quick divorce, if one is granted at all. She also learns that there is no chance of becoming like everyone else.

Orphaned as a child, Ellen Mingott was raised by her aunt in New York's high society. She has never felt at home among the elite, and instead prefers to surround herself with artists and musicians. Her eclectic taste in clothing and décor is out of step with those around her and she takes no interest in what is in or out of fashion. Even more, she speaks her mind and comes and goes as she pleases, paying no attention to social etiquette.

While back in New York, Ellen spends a lot of time with her family and her childhood friend, Newland Archer. Newland is quick to tell her that she'll never be like everybody else and he secretly prays that he is right. Newland thinks Ellen Olenska is more lovely and intriguing than any woman he has ever known—including his fiancée, May, who happens to be Ellen's cousin. Ellen and Newland's bond grows stronger until they finally admit their love to one another. Now, Ellen finds herself torn between what she feels is right in her heart and what she knows is best for her family.

What Makes Countess Ellen Olenska So Memorable?

Countess Ellen Olenska is among the most striking characters Edith Wharton created. Her plight for independence makes her easy to sympathize for, yet it is hard to ever really know her. She is a bit of a mystery. Her elusive and ambivalent nature baffles the beau monde and endears her to everyone else. What is known about her—her eclectic style, her love for art, and her desire to live without pretension— is captivating. What we don't know about her—her past with the Count, her life beyond Newland, and her deepest feeling—is even more intriguing.

The Life and Times of Edith Wharton

Like Ellen Olenska, Edith (Newbold Jones) Wharton was born into high society New York to a family that was already considered "old money" in America in 1862. She knew all the secrets of the city's elite and it's clear she enjoyed poking fun at them. When she was twenty-three, she married Edward (Teddy) Wharton, a banker twelve years older than she was. It is no secret that the marriage was a mistake; she wrote often of her marital problems in her diary. Her unhappiness led to a nervous breakdown and her doctor suggested she write as a way to help her recover. (This was a common form of therapy.) Her therapeutic writing resulted in her first book titled *The Decoration of Houses*, an architectural and home decorating book published in 1897. Eight years later, she published her first novel, *House of Mirth*.

Wharton finally put an end to her miserable marriage and divorced Edward in 1913. After that, she decided to move to France, which is where she lived for the rest of her life. In 1921, Wharton did something no woman writer had ever done—she won the Pulitzer Prize for *The Age of Innocence*. She continued to write even when she became ill and had to lie in bed most days. She published her autobiography, *A Backwards Glance*, in 1934—just three years before she died.

FROM *Age of Innocence*

It was generally agreed in New York that the Countess Olenska had "lost her looks."

She had appeared there first, in Newland Archer's boyhood, as a brilliantly pretty little girl of nine or ten, of whom people said that she "ought to be painted." Her parents had been continental wanderers, and after a roaming babyhood she had lost them both, and been taken in charge by her aunt, Medora Manson, also a wanderer, who was herself returning to New York to "settle down."

* * *

Novel Knowledge: A STEAMY AFFAIR

Edith had a lengthy love affair with Morton Fullerton, a journalist for the *London Times*. Her diary reveals the joy she felt in this passionate relationship and the painful absence of such passion in her marriage.

These things passed through Newland Archer's mind a week later as he watched the Countess Olenska enter the van der Luyden drawing-room on the evening of the momentous dinner. The occasion was a solemn one, and he wondered a little nervously how she would carry it off. She came rather late, one hand still ungloved, and fastening a bracelet about her wrist; yet she entered without any appearance of haste or embarrassment the drawing-room in which New York's most chosen company was somewhat awfully assembled.

In the middle of the room she paused, looking about her with a grave mouth and smiling eyes; and in that instant Newland Archer rejected the general verdict on her looks. It was true that her early radiance was gone. The red cheeks had paled; she was thin, worn, a little older-looking than her age, which must have been nearly thirty. But there was about her the mysterious authority of beauty, a sureness in the carriage of the head, the movement of the eyes, which, without being in the least theatrical, struck his as highly trained and full of a conscious power. At the same time she was simpler in manner than most of the ladies present, and many people (as he heard afterward from Janey) were disappointed that her appearance was not more "stylish"— for stylishness was what New York most valued. It was, perhaps, Archer reflected, because her early vivacity had disappeared; because she was so quiet—quiet in her movements, her voice, and the tones of her low-pitched voice. New York had expected something a good deal more resonant in a young woman with such a history.

* * *

Madame Olenska did not move when he came up behind her, and for a second their eyes met in the mirror; then she turned, threw herself into her sofa-corner, and sighed out: "There's time for a cigarette."

He handed her the box and lit a spill for her; and as the flame flashed up into her face she glanced at him with laughing eyes and said: "What do you think of me in a temper?"

Archer paused a moment; then he answered with sudden resolution: "It makes me understand what your aunt has been saying about you."

"I knew she'd been talking about me. Well?"

"She said you were used to all kinds of things—splendours and amusements and excitements—that we could never hope to give you here."

Madame Olenska smiled faintly into the circle of smoke about her lips.

"Medora is incorrigibly romantic. It has made up to her for so many things!"

Novel Knowledge: EDITH'S CRUSADE

During World War I, Edith worked to aid refugees from northeastern France and Belgium. She raised money to build schools and start programs to help employ women.

Archer hesitated again, and again took his risk. "Is your aunt's romanticism always consistent with accuracy?"

"You mean: does she speak the truth?" Her niece considered. "Well, I'll tell you: in almost everything she says, there's something true and something untrue. But why do you ask? What has she been telling you?"

He looked away into the fire, and then back at her shining presence. His heart tightened with the thought that this was their last evening by that fireside, and that in a moment the carriage would come to carry her away.

"She says—she pretends that Count Olenski has asked her to persuade you to go back to him."

Madame Olenska made no answer. She sat motionless, holding her cigarette in her half-lifted hand. The expression of her face had not changed; and Archer remembered that he had before noticed her apparent incapacity for surprise.

"You knew, then?" he broke out.

She was silent for so long that the ash dropped from her cigarette. She brushed it to the floor. "She has hinted about a letter: poor darling! Medora's hints—"

"Is it at your husband's request that she has arrived here suddenly?"

Madame Olenska seemed to consider this question also. "There again: one can't tell. She told me she had had a 'spiritual summons,' whatever that is, from Dr. Carver. I'm afraid she's going to marry Dr. Carver . . . poor Medora, there's always some one she wants to marry. But perhaps the people in Cuba just got tired of her! I think she was with them as a sort of paid companion. Really, I don't know why she came."

"But you do believe she has a letter from your husband?"

Again Madame Olenska brooded silently; then she said: "After all, it was to be expected."

The young man rose and went to lean against the fireplace. A sudden restlessness possessed him, and he was tongue-tied by the sense that their minutes were numbered, and that at any moment he might hear the wheels of the returning carriage.

"You know that your aunt believes you will go back?"

Madame Olenska raised her head quickly. A deep blush rose to her face and spread over her neck and shoulders. She blushed seldom and painfully, as if it hurt her like a burn.

"Many cruel things have been believed of me," she said.

"Oh, Ellen—forgive me; I'm a fool and a brute!"

She smiled a little. "You are horribly nervous; you have your own troubles. I know you think the Wellands are unreasonable about your marriage, and of course I agree with you. In Europe people don't understand our long American engagements; I suppose they are not as calm as we are." She pronounced the "we" with a faint emphasis that gave it an ironic sound.

Archer felt the irony but did not dare to take it up. After all, she had perhaps purposely deflected the conversation from her own affairs, and after the pain his last words had evidently caused her he felt that all he could do was to follow her lead. But the sense of the waning hour made him desperate: he could not bear the thought that a barrier of words should drop between them again.

"Yes," he said abruptly; "I went south to ask May to marry me after Easter. There's no reason why we shouldn't be married then."

"And May adores you—and yet you couldn't convince her? I thought her too intelligent to be the slave of such absurd superstitions."

"She IS too intelligent—she's not their slave."

Madame Olenska looked at him. "Well, then—I don't understand."

Archer reddened, and hurried on with a rush. "We had a frank talk—almost the first. She thinks my impatience a bad sign."

"Merciful heavens—a bad sign?"

"She thinks it means that I can't trust myself to go on caring for her. She thinks, in short, I want to marry her at once to get away from some one that I—care for more."

Madame Olenska examined this curiously. "But if she thinks that—why isn't she in a hurry too?"

"Because she's not like that: she's so much nobler. She insists all the more on the long engagement, to give me time—"

"Time to give her up for the other woman?"

"If I want to."

Madame Olenska leaned toward the fire and gazed into it with fixed eyes. Down the quiet street Archer heard the approaching trot of her horses.

"That IS noble," she said, with a slight break in her voice.

"Yes. But it's ridiculous."

"Ridiculous? Because you don't care for any one else?"

"Because I don't mean to marry any one else."

"Ah." There was another long interval. At length she looked up at him and asked: "This other woman—does she love you?"

"Oh, there's no other woman; I mean, the person that May was thinking of is—was never—"

"Then, why, after all, are you in such haste?"

"There's your carriage," said Archer.

She half-rose and looked about her with absent eyes. Her fan and gloves lay on the sofa beside her and she picked them up mechanically.

"Yes; I suppose I must be going."

"You're going to Mrs. Struthers's?"

"Yes." She smiled and added: "I must go where I am invited, or I should be too lonely. Why not come with me?"

Archer felt that at any cost he must keep her beside him, must make her give him the rest of her evening. Ignoring her question, he continued to lean against the chimney-piece, his eyes fixed on the hand in which she held her gloves and fan, as if watching to see if he had the power to make her drop them.

"May guessed the truth," he said. "There is another woman—but not the one she thinks."

Ellen Olenska made no answer, and did not move. After a moment he sat down beside her, and, taking her hand, softly unclasped it, so that the gloves and fan fell on the sofa between them.

She started up, and freeing herself from him moved away to the other side of the hearth. "Ah, don't make love to me! Too many people have done that," she said, frowning.

Archer, changing colour, stood up also: it was the bitterest rebuke she could have given him. "I have never made love to you," he said, "and I never shall. But you are the woman I would have married if it had been possible for either of us."

"Possible for either of us?" She looked at him with unfeigned astonishment. "And you say that—when it's you who've made it impossible?"

He stared at her, groping in a blackness through which a single arrow of light tore its blinding way.

"I'VE made it impossible—?"

"You, you, YOU!" she cried, her lip trembling like a child's on the verge of tears. "Isn't it you who made me give up divorcing—give it up because you showed me how selfish and wicked it was, how one must sacrifice one's self to preserve the dignity of marriage . . . and to spare one's family the publicity, the scandal? And because my family was going to be your family—for May's sake and for yours—I did what you told me, what you proved to me that I ought to do. Ah," she broke out with a sudden laugh, "I've made no secret of having done it for you!"

She sank down on the sofa again, crouching among the festive ripples of her dress like a stricken masquerader; and the young man stood by the fireplace and continued to gaze at her without moving.

"Good God," he groaned. "When I thought—"

"You thought?"

"Ah, don't ask me what I thought!"

Still looking at her, he saw the same burning flush creep up her neck to her face. She sat upright, facing him with a rigid dignity.

"I do ask you."

"Well, then: there were things in that letter you asked me to read—"

"My husband's letter?"

"Yes."

"I had nothing to fear from that letter: absolutely nothing! All I feared was to bring notoriety, scandal, on the family—on you and May."

"Good God," he groaned again, bowing his face in his hands.

The silence that followed lay on them with the weight of things final and irrevocable. It seemed to Archer to be crushing him down like his own grave-stone; in all the wide future he saw nothing that would ever lift that load from his heart. He did not move from his place, or raise his head from his hands; his hidden eyeballs went on staring into utter darkness.

"At least I loved you—" he brought out.

On the other side of the hearth, from the sofa-corner where he supposed that she still crouched, he heard a faint stifled crying like a child's. He started up and came to her side.

"Ellen! What madness! Why are you crying? Nothing's done that can't be undone. I'm still free, and you're going to be." He had her in his arms, her face like a wet flower at his lips, and all their vain terrors shrivelling up like ghosts at sunrise. The one thing that astonished him now was that he should have stood for five minutes arguing with her across the width of the room, when just touching her made everything so simple.

She gave him back all his kiss, but after a moment he felt her stiffening in his arms, and she put him aside and stood up.

"Ah, my poor Newland—I suppose this had to be. But it doesn't in the least alter things," she said, looking down at him in her turn from the hearth.

"It alters the whole of life for me."

"No, no—it mustn't, it can't. You're engaged to May Welland; and I'm married."

He stood up too, flushed and resolute. "Nonsense! It's too late for that sort of thing. We've no right to lie to other people or to ourselves. We won't talk of your marriage; but do you see me marrying May after this?"

She stood silent, resting her thin elbows on the mantelpiece, her profile reflected in the glass behind her. One of the locks of her chignon had become loosened and hung on her neck; she looked haggard and almost old.

"I don't see you," she said at length, "putting that question to May. Do you?"

He gave a reckless shrug. "It's too late to do anything else."

"You say that because it's the easiest thing to say at this moment—
not because it's true. In reality it's too late to do anything but what
we'd both decided on."

"Ah, I don't understand you!"

She forced a pitiful smile that pinched her face instead of smoothing it. "You don't understand because you haven't yet guessed how
you've changed things for me: oh, from the first—long before I
knew all you'd done."

"All I'd done?"

"Yes. I was perfectly unconscious at first that people here were
shy of me—that they thought I was a dreadful sort of person. It
seems they had even refused to meet me at dinner. I found that
out afterward; and how you'd made your mother go with you to
the van der Luydens'; and how you'd insisted on announcing your
engagement at the Beaufort ball, so that I might have two families
to stand by me instead of one—"

At that he broke into a laugh.

"Just imagine," she said, "how stupid and unobservant I was! I
knew nothing of all this till Granny blurted it out one day. New
York simply meant peace and freedom to me: it was coming home.
And I was so happy at being among my own people that every one
I met seemed kind and good, and glad to see me. But from the
very beginning," she continued, "I felt there was no one as kind
as you; no one who gave me reasons that I understood for doing
what at first seemed so hard and—unnecessary. The very good
people didn't convince me; I felt they'd never been tempted. But
you knew; you understood; you had felt the world outside tugging

at one with all its golden hands—and yet you hated the things it asks of one; you hated happiness bought by disloyalty and cruelty and indifference. That was what I'd never known before—and it's better than anything I've known."

She spoke in a low even voice, without tears or visible agitation; and each word, as it dropped from her, fell into his breast like burning lead. He sat bowed over, his head between his hands, staring at the hearthrug, and at the tip of the satin shoe that showed under her dress. Suddenly he knelt down and kissed the shoe.

She bent over him, laying her hands on his shoulders, and looking at him with eyes so deep that he remained motionless under her gaze.

"Ah, don't let us undo what you've done!" she cried. "I can't go back now to that other way of thinking. I can't love you unless I give you up."

His arms were yearning up to her; but she drew away, and they remained facing each other, divided by the distance that her words had created. Then, abruptly, his anger overflowed.

Clarissa Dalloway

IN *THE VOYAGE OUT* BY VIRGINA WOOLF
FIRST PUBLISHED IN: 1915

Who is she? A high-spirited, charming woman who takes the spotlight whenever she walks into the room.

Her Story

Clarissa and her husband Richard Dalloway are traveling abroad in Lisbon when they board a ship headed to South America. It's there that they meet fellow passenger Rachel Vicane, a young, sheltered woman who is learning the sorts of things her father has tried so hard to shield her from. The voyage brings romance for Rachel, and a lot of life's hard-to-escape lessons and questions. While *The Voyage Out* is supposed to be Rachel's story, Clarissa is the most memorable character on the ship. Like all who meet her, Rachel is captivated by Clarissa's independent spirit, her worldliness, her ability to move about a room with such confidence, and perhaps most of all, the way she speaks her mind and seems to have something intelligent to say on any given topic. Despite Mr. Dalloway's efforts to make a strong impression on Rachel (he even kisses her) his wife is the one who leaves a lasting effect. In just a few chapters, Clarissa Dalloway influences Rachel and the other passengers so strongly that she is talked about and missed long after the goodbyes.

What Makes Clarissa Dalloway So Memorable?

Clarissa Dalloway is a woman of high society who has figured out how to be dependent on a husband for everything she needs in life, yet is independent in mind and spirit. Her lively personality takes over a room and raises the level of conversation at any party. She asks questions that hint at a broader knowledge on most subjects and she inquires with an orneriness that keeps people on their toes. She revels in life, even the challenges life often brings, and her energy draws people to her. Perhaps her most memorable quality, however, is the deeper understanding she has about life and the importance of happiness—however one chooses to define it. We catch a glimpse of this trait in *The Voyage Out*, just enough to want more. We see it more acutely in the novel that bears her name.

The Life and Times of Virgina Woolf

Virginia Woolf was born in London in 1882 as Adeline Virginia Stephen. Though the family lived in London, her fondest childhood memories were from her summers spent in St. Ives in Cromwell where her family had a summer home. However, those sunny memories started to fade as she entered her teens. Thirteen was a terrible age for her. First, her mother died. Then, that same year, she had her first of many nervous breakdowns. Two years later her half-sister died.

Novel Knowledge: LASTING IMPRESSION

Clarissa Dalloway proved so memorable to readers that Virginia Woolf decided to devote a novel to the character ten years after she was introduced in *The Voyage Out*. During the years between, readers saw Clarissa Dalloway in the short story, "Mrs Dalloway in Bond Street." Today, Clarissa Dalloway is Woolf's most well-known and most analyzed character.

When Woolf's father died in 1904, she was briefly placed in a mental hospital. Her mind never fully recovered and she dealt with depression for the rest of her life.

In 1912, she married a "penniless Jew," at least that is how she described Leonard Woolf. The marriage was for love and nothing else. In 1937 she wrote in her diary: "Love-making—after 25 years can't bear to be separate . . . you see it is enormous pleasure being wanted: a wife. And our marriage so complete." Together, the couple founded Hogarth Press in 1917. Hogarth published her novels along with works by T. S. Eliot and other literary giants.

Woolf's work was often considered elitist and appealed to a narrow audience. But the feminist movement in the 1960s brought her to the forefront of literature again. Leonard was supportive of his wife's writing, but it seemed there was little he could do to help her fight depression. After finishing her novel, *Between the Acts*, she fell into a deep depression again. World War I had destroyed her home in London and the poor reviews she earned from a biography she wrote on a dear old friend, Roger Fry, seemed to only add to her depression. She could no longer write, nor could she manage to think clearly. In March of 1941, Woolf wrote a goodbye letter to her husband before filling her coat with rocks and drowning herself in a nearby river. Her body was found three weeks after her death.

From *The Voyage Out*

Next morning Clarissa was up before anyone else. She dressed, and was out on deck, breathing the fresh air of a calm morning, and, making the circuit of the ship for the second time, she ran straight into the lean person of Mr. Grice, the steward. She apologised, and at the same time asked him to enlighten her: what were those shiny brass stands for, half glass on the top? She had been wondering, and could not guess. When he had done explaining, she cried enthusiastically:

"I do think that to be a sailor must be the finest thing in the world!"

"And what d'you know about it?" said Mr. Grice, kindling in a strange manner. "Pardon me. What does any man or woman brought up in England know about the sea? They profess to know; but they don't."

The bitterness with which he spoke was ominous of what was to come. He led her off to his own quarters, and, sitting on the edge of a brass-bound table, looking uncommonly like a sea-gull, with her white tapering body and thin alert face, Mrs. Dalloway had to listen to the tirade of a fanatical man. Did she realise, to begin with, what a very small part of the world the land was? How peaceful, how beautiful, how benignant in comparison the sea? The deep waters could sustain Europe unaided if every earthly animal died of the plague to-morrow. Mr. Grice recalled dreadful sights which he had seen in the richest city of the world—men and women standing in line hour after hour to receive a mug of greasy soup. "And I thought of the good flesh down here waiting and asking to be caught. I'm not exactly a Protestant, and I'm not a Catholic, but I could almost pray for the days of popery to come again—because of the fasts."

As he talked he kept opening drawers and moving little glass jars. Here were the treasures which the great ocean had bestowed upon him—pale fish in greenish liquids, blobs of jelly with streaming tresses, fish with lights in their heads, they lived so deep.

"They have swum about among bones," Clarissa sighed.

"You're thinking of Shakespeare," said Mr. Grice, and taking down a copy from a shelf well lined with books, recited in an emphatic nasal voice:

"Full fathom five thy father lies, "A grand fellow, Shakespeare," he said, replacing the volume.

Clarissa was so glad to hear him say so.

"Which is your favourite play? I wonder if it's the same as mine?"

"*Henry the Fifth*," said Mr. Grice.

"Joy!" cried Clarissa. "It is!"

Hamlet was what you might call too introspective for Mr. Grice, the sonnets too passionate; *Henry the Fifth* was to him the model of an English gentleman. But his favourite reading was Huxley, Herbert Spencer, and Henry George; while Emerson and Thomas Hardy he read for relaxation. He was giving Mrs. Dalloway his views upon the present state of England when the breakfast bell rung so imperiously that she had to tear herself away, promising to come back and be shown his sea-weeds.

Novel Knowledge: A MOTHER'S BEAUTY

Virgina's mother, Julia Prinsep Stephen, was a descendant of one of Marie Antoinette's ladies in waiting. Known for her beauty, Julia modeled for Pre-Ralphaelist painters such as Edward Burnes-Jones.

The party, which had seemed so odd to her the night before, was already gathered round the table, still under the influence of sleep, and therefore uncommunicative, but her entrance sent a little flutter like a breath of air through them all.

"I've had the most interesting talk of my life!" she exclaimed, taking her seat beside Willoughby. "D'you realise that one of your men is a philosopher and a poet?"

"A very interesting fellow—that's what I always say," said Willoughby, distinguishing Mr. Grice. "Though Rachel finds him a bore."

"He's a bore when he talks about currents," said Rachel. Her eyes were full of sleep, but Mrs. Dalloway still seemed to her wonderful.

"I've never met a bore yet!" said Clarissa.

"And I should say the world was full of them!" exclaimed Helen. But her beauty, which was radiant in the morning light, took the contrariness from her words.

"I agree that it's the worst one can possibly say of any one," said Clarissa. "How much rather one would be a murderer than a bore!" she added, with her usual air of saying something profound. "One can fancy liking a murderer. It's the same with dogs. Some dogs are awful bores, poor dears."

It happened that Richard was sitting next to Rachel. She was curiously conscious of his presence and appearance—his well-cut clothes, his crackling shirt-front, his cuffs with blue rings round them, and the square-tipped, very clean fingers with the red stone on the little finger of the left hand.

"We had a dog who was a bore and knew it," he said, addressing her in cool, easy tones. "He was a Skye terrier, one of those long chaps, with little feet poking out from their hair like—like caterpillars— no, like sofas I should say. Well, we had another dog at the same time, a black brisk animal—a Schipperke, I think, you call them. You can't imagine a greater contrast. The Skye so slow and deliberate, looking up at you like some old gentleman in the club, as much as to say, 'You don't really mean it, do you?' and the Schipperke as quick as a knife. I liked the Skye best, I must confess. There was something pathetic about him."

The story seemed to have no climax.

"What happened to him?" Rachel asked.

"That's a very sad story," said Richard, lowering his voice and peeling an apple. "He followed my wife in the car one day and got run over by a brute of a cyclist."

"Was he killed?" asked Rachel.

But Clarissa at her end of the table had overheard.

"Don't talk of it!" she cried. "It's a thing I can't bear to think of to this day."

Surely the tears stood in her eyes?

"That's the painful thing about pets," said Mr. Dalloway; "they die. The first sorrow I can remember was for the death of a dormouse. I regret to say that I sat upon it. Still, that didn't make one any the less sorry. Here lies the duck that Samuel Johnson sat on, eh? I was big for my age."

"Then we had canaries," he continued, "a pair of ring-doves, a lemur, and at one time a martin."

"Did you live in the country?" Rachel asked him.

"We lived in the country for six months of the year. When I say 'we' I mean four sisters, a brother, and myself. There's nothing like coming of a large family. Sisters particularly are delightful."

"Dick, you were horribly spoilt!" cried Clarissa across the table.

"No, no. Appreciated," said Richard.

Rachel had other questions on the tip of her tongue; or rather one enormous question, which she did not in the least know how to put into words. The talk appeared too airy to admit of it.

"Please tell me—everything." That was what she wanted to say. He had drawn apart one little chink and showed astonishing treasures. It seemed to her incredible that a man like that should be willing to talk to her. He had sisters and pets, and once lived in the country. She stirred her tea round and round; the bubbles which swam and clustered in the cup seemed to her like the union of their minds.

The talk meanwhile raced past her, and when Richard suddenly stated in a jocular tone of voice, "I'm sure Miss Vinrace, now, has secret leanings towards Catholicism," she had no idea what to answer, and Helen could not help laughing at the start she gave.

However, breakfast was over and Mrs. Dalloway was rising. "I always think religion's like collecting beetles," she said, summing up the discussion as she went up the stairs with Helen. "One person has a passion for black beetles; another hasn't; it's no good arguing about it. What's *your* black beetle now?"

"I suppose it's my children," said Helen.

"Ah—that's different," Clarissa breathed. "Do tell me. You have a boy, haven't you? Isn't it detestable, leaving them?"

It was as though a blue shadow had fallen across a pool. Their eyes became deeper, and their voices more cordial. Instead of joining them as they began to pace the deck, Rachel was indignant with the prosperous matrons, who made her feel outside their world and motherless, and turning back, she left them abruptly. She slammed the door of her room, and pulled out her music. It was all old music—Bach and Beethoven, Mozart and Purcell—the pages yellow, the engraving rough to the finger. In three minutes she was deep in a very difficult, very classical fugue in A, and over her face came a queer remote impersonal expression of complete absorption and anxious satisfaction. Now she stumbled; now she faltered and had to play the same bar twice over; but an invisible line seemed to string the notes together, from which rose a shape, a building. She was so far absorbed in this work, for it was really difficult to find how all these sounds should stand together, and drew upon the whole of her faculties, that she never heard a knock at the door. It was burst impulsively open, and Mrs. Dalloway stood in the room leaving the door open, so that a strip of the white deck and of the blue sea appeared through the opening. The shape of the Bach fugue crashed to the ground.

"Don't let me interrupt," Clarissa implored. "I heard you playing, and I couldn't resist. I adore Bach!"

Rachel flushed and fumbled her fingers in her lap. She stood up awkwardly.

"It's too difficult," she said.

"But you were playing quite splendidly! I ought to have stayed outside."

"No," said Rachel.

She slid *Cowper's Letters* and *Wuthering Heights* out of the armchair, so that Clarissa was invited to sit there.

"What a dear little room!" she said, looking round. "Oh, *Cowper's Letters*! I've never read them. Are they nice?"

"Rather dull," said Rachel.

"He wrote awfully well, didn't he?" said Clarissa; "—if one likes that kind of thing—finished his sentences and all that. *Wuthering Heights*! Ah—that's more in my line. I really couldn't exist without the Brontës. Don't you love them? Still, on the whole, I'd rather live without them than without Jane Austen."

Lightly and at random though she spoke, her manner conveyed an extraordinary degree of sympathy and desire to befriend.

"Jane Austen? I don't like Jane Austen," said Rachel.

"You monster!" Clarissa exclaimed. "I can only just forgive you. Tell me why?"

"She's so—so—well, so like a tight plait," Rachel floundered.

"Ah—I see what you mean. But I don't agree. And you won't when you're older. At your age I only liked Shelley. I can remember sobbing over him in the garden.

He has outsoared the shadow of our night,

Envy and calumny and hate and pain—you remember?

Can touch him not and torture not again

From the contagion of the world's slow stain.

How divine!—and yet what nonsense!" She looked lightly round the room. "I always think it's *living*, not dying, that counts. I really respect some snuffy old stockbroker who's gone on adding up column after column all his days, and trotting back to his villa at Brixton with some old pug dog he worships, and a dreary little wife sitting at the end of the table, and going off to Margate for a fortnight—I assure you I know heaps like that—well, they seem to me *really* nobler than poets whom every one worships, just because they're geniuses and die young. But I don't expect *you* to agree with me!"

She pressed Rachel's shoulder.

"Um-m-m—" she went on quoting—

Unrest which men miscall delight—

"When you're my age you'll see that the world is *crammed* with delightful things. I think young people make such a mistake about that—not letting themselves be happy. I sometimes think that happiness is the only thing that counts. I don't know you well enough to say, but I should guess you might be a little inclined to—when one's young and attractive—I'm going to say it!—*every*thing's at one's feet." She glanced round as much as to say, "not only a few stuffy books and Bach."

"I long to ask questions," she continued. "You interest me so much. If I'm impertinent, you must just box my ears."

"And I—I want to ask questions," said Rachel with such earnestness that Mrs. Dalloway had to check her smile.

"D'you mind if we walk?" she said. "The air's so delicious."

She snuffed it like a racehorse as they shut the door and stood on deck.

"Isn't it good to be alive?" she exclaimed, and drew Rachel's arm within hers.

"Look, look! How exquisite!"

The shores of Portugal were beginning to lose their substance; but the land was still the land, though at a great distance. They could distinguish the little towns that were sprinkled in the folds of the hills, and the smoke rising faintly. The towns appeared to be very small in comparison with the great purple mountains behind them.

"Honestly, though," said Clarissa, having looked, "I don't like views. They're too inhuman." They walked on.

"How odd it is!" she continued impulsively. "This time yesterday we'd never met. I was packing in a stuffy little room in the hotel. We know absolutely nothing about each other—and yet—I feel as if I *did* know you!"

"You have children—your husband was in Parliament?"

"You've never been to school, and you live——?"

"With my aunts at Richmond."

"Richmond?"

"You see, my aunts like the Park. They like the quiet."

"And you don't! I understand!" Clarissa laughed.

"I like walking in the Park alone; but not—with the dogs," she finished.

"No; and some people *are* dogs; aren't they?" said Clarissa, as if she had guessed a secret. "But not every one—oh no, not every one."

"Not every one," said Rachel, and stopped.

"I can quite imagine you walking alone," said Clarissa: "and thinking—in a little world of your own. But how you will enjoy it—some day!"

"I shall enjoy walking with a man—is that what you mean?" said Rachel, regarding Mrs. Dalloway with her large enquiring eyes.

"I wasn't thinking of a man particularly," said Clarissa. "But you will."

"No. I shall never marry," Rachel determined.

"I shouldn't be so sure of that," said Clarissa. Her sidelong glance told Rachel that she found her attractive although she was inexplicably amused.

"Why do people marry?" Rachel asked.

"That's what you're going to find out," Clarissa laughed.

Rachel followed her eyes and found that they rested for a second, on the robust figure of Richard Dalloway, who was engaged in striking a match on the sole of his boot; while Willoughby expounded something, which seemed to be of great interest to them both.

"There's nothing like it," she concluded. "Do tell me about the Ambroses. Or am I asking too many questions?"

"I find you easy to talk to," said Rachel.

The short sketch of the Ambroses was, however, somewhat perfunctory, and contained little but the fact that Mr. Ambrose was her uncle.

"Your mother's brother?"

When a name has dropped out of use, the lightest touch upon it tells. Mrs. Dalloway went on:

"Are you like your mother?"

"No; she was different," said Rachel.

She was overcome by an intense desire to tell Mrs. Dalloway things she had never told any one—things she had not realised herself until this moment.

"I am lonely," she began. "I want—" She did not know what she wanted, so that she could not finish the sentence; but her lip quivered.

But it seemed that Mrs. Dalloway was able to understand without words.

"I know," she said, actually putting one arm round Rachel's shoulder. "When I was your age I wanted too. No one understood until I met Richard. He gave me all I wanted. He's man and woman as well." Her eyes rested upon Mr. Dalloway, leaning upon the rail, still talking. "Don't think I say that because I'm his wife—I see his faults more clearly than I see any one else's. What one wants in the person one lives with is that they should keep one at one's best. I often wonder what I've done to be so happy!" she exclaimed, and a tear slid down her cheek. She wiped it away, squeezed Rachel's hand, and exclaimed:

"How good life is!" At that moment, standing out in the fresh breeze, with the sun upon the waves, and Mrs. Dalloway's hand upon her arm, it seemed indeed as if life which had been unnamed before was infinitely wonderful, and too good to be true.

About the Author

Jamie Cox Robertson holds a master's degree in literature and lectures at Suffolk University in Boston. She has designed and taught literary seminars for the OASIS Institute, a nationwide adult education organization, and taught literature and writing at Webster University, the Chautauqua Institute, and the Cambridge Adult Education Center in Cambridge, Massachusetts. In addition, Robertson was the founding editor of *Southern Literary Review*, *www.southernlitreview.com*, an online source for quality southern fiction. She is also the author of *A Literary Paris*. Jamie lives in Boston and Tucson with her husband and daughter.